ESCHATOLOGY
Shouldn't Be a Fightin' Word!

Fred DeRuvo

www.studygrowknow.com

Eschatology Shouldn't Be a Fightin' Word!

Copyright © 2010 by Study-Grow-Know

All rights reserved. Written permission must be secured from the publisher to use or reproduce any part of this book, except brief quotations in critical reviews or articles.

Published in Scotts Valley, California, by Study-Grow-Know
www.studygrowknow.com • www.rightly-dividing.com • www.adroitpublications.com

Scripture quotations are from The Holy Bible, English Standard Version®, copyright © 2001 by Crossway Bibles, a publishing ministry of Good News Publishers. Used by permission. All rights reserved.

Images used in this publication (unless otherwise noted) are from clipartconnection.com and used with permission, ©2007 JUPITERIMAGES, and its licensors. All rights reserved.

All Woodcuts used herein are in the Public Domain and free of copyright.

All Figure illustrations used in this book were created by the author and protected under copyright laws, © 2010.

Cover Design: Fred DeRuvo

Edited by: Hannah Richards

Library of Congress Cataloging-in-Publication Data

DeRuvo, Fred, 1957 –

ISBN 0982644388
EAN-13 9780982644386

1. Religion – Christian Theology - Eschatology

Eschatology Shouldn't Be a Fightin' Word!

Contents

Foreword: 5
    Chapter 1: Why the Fuss About the Rapture? 9
    Chapter 2: The Holy Spirit Taught Me 15
    Chapter 3: What Is Paul Saying? 31
    Chapter 4: The Agony of Disappointment 40
    Chapter 5: "Make It Go Away!" 71
    Chapter 6: I'm Not Afraid! (Much) 77
    Chapter 7: Why Not Preterists? 95
    Chapter 8: Anybody Really Know What Time It Is? 99
    Chapter 9: What Covenant? 107
    Chapter 10: Oh, *That* Covenant 113
    Chapter 11: What Is Spiritually Mature? 134
    Chapter 12: What Is An Authentic Christian? 139
    Chapter 13: One Final Thought 147
Resources for Your Library 149

*In **every thing** give thanks: for this is the will of God
in Christ Jesus concerning you.*

– 1 Thessalonians 5:18 (KJV, emphasis added)

FOREWORD

Update: This book was originally published under the title "Death or Rapture: Either Way It'll Be Your Last Day." I felt that the title was not quite accurate enough to represent what I covered inside. Therefore, with that in mind, the title changed to offer a more accurate reflection of the text and the overall purpose in writing this book. – F. DeRuvo (October 22, 2010)

Not long ago, I completed what I thought was my last book for a while: *Christianity, Practically Speaking*. I was looking forward to taking the time to create more podcasts and video lessons. However, it became clear that there was another book that I needed to get working on, with a concept that I had briefly touched on previously in one other book.

The belief of many that we are approaching the Tribulation period has foisted the discussions concerning Eschatology to the forefront. It is unheard of today to pick up a Christian publication – book, magazine, or newsletter – or spend any time on the Internet without encountering a topic related to the biblical End Times. In fact, *not* coming across these types of articles and discussions would be a surprise.

That said, though, there also seems to be a *greater* degree of rancor and animosity these days. More and more people believe that they have the answer and they "know" they have the answer because they "prayed that the Holy Spirit would guide them into the truth they were seeking." Interestingly enough no one seems to notice that almost everyone who has offered their opinion about Eschatology makes this claim, in spite of the fact that many differing opinions exist concerning the same passages of Scripture.

Obviously, the Holy Spirit cannot be teaching everyone with opposing viewpoints simply because they prayed that He would do so. Something somewhere along the line did not pan out; however, it is doubtful that you will ever hear anyone say, "*I could be wrong*," or "*in my opinion*," or something similar. Opinions are normally stated as fact, not opinion.

Because of all this, what remains is that somehow, somewhere, many Christians seem to have fallen down on the job. In their pursuit of the truth of Eschatology, multitudes of Christians have become adept at finger pointing, accusing one another, and denouncing the Eschatological beliefs of others with whom they disagree. This is often meted out with a grand display of sanctimony that should *not* exist within the Church, but does. All of this has brought me to the conclusion that attitudes between Christians could be far better, and I include *myself* in this grouping. This particular book, which I believe offers something that has not been stated, or has not been stated loudly *enough*, is the result.

While it is unequivocally necessary *and* beneficial to study and discuss the End Times, it is completely *unnecessary* to elevate these portions of Scripture to a position higher than one's need for salvation. It appears as though this is where we have come to, with the Great Commission taking a back seat to prophecy. It seems that at this point, we might hear from Paul the words, "*Brothers, this ought not to be!*" Yet it is the case, and we have only ourselves to blame. Granted, there are without doubt individuals within the visible Church who are nothing more than what Jesus called "tares." They are in the visible Church because Satan has placed them there and their mission is to disrupt at any cost by creating disharmony and dissension.

Please understand what I am stating. I firmly believe that the study *and* discussion of Eschatology is beneficial for any number of reasons. Our Lord obviously spent time teaching it and discussing it, so that is reason enough. As the Christian studies Eschatology, our mind begins to focus on *heavenly* things and we begin to long for the return of our God and King Jesus, who will right wrongs and rule with perfect justice. As we focus more and more on *Him* and His return, we become purified, as we are told in 1 John 3, because we are focusing on things that are above.

For those of you who have spent time studying prophecy and the End Times, would you not agree that there is frequently a tremendous amount of rancor, often coming to the fore as name-calling and labeling? People are often labeled as "deceived" because of a particular view of the Rapture they support, for instance. Some are labeled heretics because of their association with what is seen as the "heresy" of Dispensationalism.

In this book, the goal is to highlight the differences (if they exist) between believing in a *PreTrib Rapture* and the *imminent death* of every person alive today. For those who believe the PreTrib Rapture has dubious origins, which in turn creates individuals who are deceived, it is important to look seriously at fact of the *imminency of death* for each of us. It must be asked what the real difference is if we compare the two.   The answer may surprise.

Is this book the definitive study for this topic? It would be nice; however, I do not kid myself into thinking that it *is* that. Either others will write an opinion in favor of, or against the position of this book, or they will ignore it altogether.

Certainly, any doctrine must be judged based on Scripture, and too often doctrines are determined to be either true or false by straw man arguments and ad hominem attacks. The bottom line, though, is that we must judge all discussion of Eschatology by comparing it to Scripture and the marching orders provided to us by the Lord Himself: *the Great Commission*. Is all the discussion about the End Times, the various views of the Rapture, the literality of the 70 weeks and more taking us all away from the one job that we were actually commissioned by our Lord to do?

Shouldn't we be spending at least as *much* time evangelizing the lost as we spend discussing areas of Eschatology? Should we stop the war of words long enough to plant some seeds, water others, and watch the harvest? Should not the major *end* goal of any discussion of Eschatology be *evangelization*?

The study of the End Times is *valuable*. However, if the result does not create a *greater* desire to evangelize the lost because of that study, then we have fallen woefully short. May the Lord bless our desire to know, as Daniel endeavored to know, the signs of the times, and may those signs create within us a burden for the lost souls of this world.

Fred DeRuvo, February 2010

Chapter 1
Why Fuss About the Rapture?

I have already written a few books on the subject of Eschatology (the study of the Last Days, or End Times), which have included *aspects* of the PreTrib Rapture with arguments *for* and *against* it. In today's biblical landscape, it seems that the situation continues to demand a hard look at Eschatology and its ramifications.

While there are many facets of Eschatology that are currently being discussed, in my own studies I have found that by far, the most acrimonious assault is directed toward those who believe in a *PreTrib Rapture*. This is the belief that Jesus will step out of the third heavens, come toward the earth, and will call His Bride up to be with Him prior to the start of the Tribulation. The Rapture is the "catching away" of believers (the dead believers first, followed by those who are alive) to heaven, which Paul speaks of in the book of 1 Thessalonians.

There are many who offer reasons against the PreTrib Rapture position, and certainly a good many of those individuals truly believe they are doing some good for all of Christendom. I believe others have done nothing more than create a virtual cesspool of rancor and hostility. This is due, in my opinion, to the fact that they themselves are so ardently opposed to the PreTrib Rapture that they believe it is their mission to destroy it at all costs.

Most are familiar with Dave MacPherson's multiple books on the subject of the Rapture. MacPherson, who is likely the godfather of the current established views against the PreTrib Rapture position, came out of the chute with guns blazing against the very idea that the PreTrib Rapture was a plausible and biblical doctrine. Certainly there were others before Dave who argued against the PreTrib Rapture, but for the most part and in this current generation, Dave has spent a good deal of time stirring up the waters. From his first book he insisted the entire belief was a preposterous cover-up, perpetrated by two individuals (J. N. Darby and C. I. Scofield) who rested their case on the word of a 15 year-old girl named Margaret MacDonald regarding the vision she allegedly had. MacPherson believes he has won the case easily, forever defeating PreTribulationalism as the lie that he certainly believes it to be. All that is left is for the PreTribber himself to admit defeat, and quietly go away with his tail tucked between his legs.

Was Margaret Pre or Posttribulation?
Because there are so many who have not only bought MacPherson's books, but have also agreed wholeheartedly with his viewpoints, hostilities toward the PreTrib Rapture and those who advocate it

have diametrically increased since his first book was published in the early 70s. In the end, one must ask whether MacPherson has actually proven anything. For instance, if one takes the time to thoroughly read the written record of MacDonald's vision, it is difficult to come away from it with the belief that MacDonald's vision actually pointed toward a *Pretribulational* view. It seems more accurate to say that her vision and resultant belief pointed toward a view that is decidedly *Posttribulational*.

There are many aspects of the PreTrib Rapture about which MacPherson has written that, in the final analysis, simply do not gel. This does not seem to matter at all to those who *believe* that he has not only found *the* response to the PreTrib Rapture position, but also *soundly* defeated it as the (alleged) deception it has come to be known.

It is because many of them simply take MacPherson's word for it that they have, by extension, become little MacPhersons. These individuals parrot his words, his arguments, and even his sarcasm. Though *they* are guilty of this, these same individuals complain loudly against the PreTribber who, it is said, merely hears and accepts verbatim what is taught by Bible college professors and pastors.

Because these folks thoroughly believe MacPherson's premise, they too believe that the PreTrib Rapture is born of deception, and since it was born of deception, then those who espouse it are by association deceived as well. Because it is believed that the PreTrib Rapturist is fully *deceived* (since MacPherson believes he has shown that this viewpoint has dubious origins and is a fabricated doctrine), then it is further believed that this same PreTrib Rapturist will likely take the mark of the beast (should he be alive when the Tribulation occurs).

It follows then that (according to the <u>anti</u>-PreTrib Rapturist) the deceived PreTribber is in need of being *freed* from their deception.

Therefore, instead of focusing on the *lost*, who do *not* know Christ, many Posttribbers and other anti-PreTribbers have begun focusing on the "deceived PreTrib Rapturist" as part of their "ministry." They try to talk to the PreTribber, hoping that the Lord will free him from his blindness. Once it is realized that nothing they say will do the trick, the PreTribber is normally seen as an enemy of the cross, with the anti-PreTribber shaking the dust from his feet and moving on to the next individual.

I realize this scenario sounds dramatic; however, I have been on the receiving end of this attitude. There have been individuals who have accosted me verbally with their words of warning and eventual "I'm-shaking-the-dust-off-my-sandals" foot shaking so that I would know, finally, that I have become anathema to the Lord.

Frankly, I believe this to be a tragic situation. Most of the individuals I personally know who also happen to be PreTribbers are godly people, serving God and endeavoring to know Christ better on a daily basis in order that He and He alone will receive glory. When I consider the works of Ryrie, Walvoord, and many others, what I am always met with is a spirit of *compassion*, *patience*, and *love*. These men are *far* from argumentative and always present their opinions as something I'm sure brings God glory, because nothing they say (that I have read) has done anything to engender an attitude of anger or haughtiness. While some might indeed *become* angered after reading Ryrie or Walvoord, it is likely they do so because they disagree with them, not because of the *way in which* these men have presented their case.

Sarcastic Rhetoric and Rejoinders
This is unfortunately *not* the case with Dave MacPherson. His books are filled with sarcastic rejoinders and remonstration toward Ryrie, Walvoord, Dr. Thomas Ice, and many other conservative, biblical scholars. The fact that MacPherson has even had the temerity to imply that Dr. Ice's doctoral degree is worthless is beyond the pale. I

realize it is difficult at times *not* to be sarcastic, especially when someone believes so strongly in his or her own position. However, sarcasm should be used in a very limited fashion if at all, due to the reaction it pulls from people. I have to admit to my own tendency toward sarcasm, and I have often gone back over my books changing or removing altogether what I at first thought was well said even though it was peppered with disdain.

This fuss about the Rapture (specifically the PreTrib version) needs to *stop*. Christians need to be people who love each other with a holy and precious love. Just because some believe the *incorrect* idea that I am wrong and therefore deceived due to my belief in the PreTrib Rapture position, it does not make *their* opinion correct, either about me or about *their* doctrinal stance. People often state their opinions as fact. I do the same thing. However, a belief that someone is wrong about an opinion does not mean he or she *is* wrong. We need to learn to stop attacking others because their opinions regarding Eschatology differ from ours. In fact, we should not attack people who do not agree that salvation is only found in Jesus Christ either. We should seek to correct in gentleness, though admittedly, that is difficult at times.

Like Posttribbers and others, I can show from Scripture how I come to my conclusions regarding the Rapture or any other doctrine I hold to be true, like the deity of Christ, the Trinity and other orthodox positions. My views should be respected, and if people disagree with my conclusions, they most certainly have a right to do so. However, they do *not* have a right to label me *deluded* or *deceived* and believe that *because* of their belief, I am in need of their deliverance ministry.

The Church needs to get back on track. Eschatology *is* important for a variety of reasons, but one of the most important reasons is focusing on the fact that one day Jesus' Kingdom will physically be among us. We had best become better equipped to evangelize the lost *today,* regardless of our Eschatological viewpoint.

If I knew that at any moment your house down the street from mine could burst into flames due to a gas leak, I would *not* be sitting on my couch watching TV, thinking that since I'm probably safe, I don't need to worry about it. I would also *not* leave your "salvation" up to the Lord, believing that He will take care of it even if I do not do anything to even attempt to save you and your family.

In fact, I would be doing everything I could to get your attention and get you *out* and *away* from the house that could soon be your grave. This is what we are called to do, and I believe more than any other biblical position out there the PreTrib Rapture position places me in the frame of mind where I realize that life *will* end, for all of us. It is predestined by God Himself.

The PreTrib Rapture *keeps* me focused on the End Times and the fact that life is very, *very* short, just as realizing that my *death* is always *imminent* does the same exact thing. It is *because* of this that I want to and endeavor to serve the Lord, bringing the Gospel of His Kingdom to those who do not yet know Him.

Chapter 2
The Holy Spirit Taught Me

Declarative statements are often made and intended to cause others to believe that the individual *making* the declarative statements does so because he has *proven* his case beyond doubt. Unfortunately, when it comes to *debate* this is rarely the case, because the final determination is in the mind of the listener, *not* the speaker.

Someone who *has* in fact proven his case might *still* find his arguments rejected by listeners. We see this numerous times in the case of Peter and Paul throughout the book of Acts. It is amazing how often people make comments like this:

"I decided to lay out my biblical understanding of this much disputed doctrine here in this blog. During my walk with God, I have flipped flopped having first believed when I went to a Tim LaHaye conference several years ago. This occurred when I was a true babe in Christ and had only just begun a sincere walk. **Subsequently...I began to read the Word myself and let the Holy Spirit guide me in all truth***."*

The above quote – especially the sentence I have bolded - is similar to many others that I have heard, and you have likely heard them as well. Even though people do not necessarily *mean* to come across this way, by itself, it is an arrogant statement to make. When someone makes that statement, what he or she is doing is claiming that *the Holy Spirit has directly taught him or her.* Conversely, the Spirit has *not* taught anyone who holds a *different* or *opposing* viewpoint. It is that simple.

This type of statement is normally made in connection with the many discussions concerning the PreTrib Rapture. However, those statements are certainly not limited to that subject. People will disparage the Bible college learning that folks who believe the PreTrib Rapture have had by making comments like *"These people just take what they are taught at Bible college verbatim and believe it, without really thinking about or studying the Scriptures on their own!"* This applies to the pastors who teach the PreTrib Rapture position as well.

Again, what is being stated is that the people who believe in a PreTrib Rapture position do so because they:

- *Do not think for themselves*
- *Trust the teaching of others without studying on their own*
- *Are not taught by the Holy Spirit*
- *Are deceived (in some cases)*

I am all for discussing aspects of theology and referring only to Scripture to support my view and to flesh out the meaning of the text. This process may also include using and/or understanding the following:

- *Word studies*
- *History*
- *Cultural jargon and idioms*
- *Context of Scripture*

Talk to the Hand

Individuals who make the type of accusations and statements noted previously are also usually the first to go outside the Bible for their "evidence" and "proof." Normally, one of the first people they run to is Dave MacPherson and any one of his eight books on the subject of the PreTrib Rapture. Apparently, Mr. MacPherson considers this topic to be of supreme importance, as I have yet to see his name associated with any work that deals specifically with salvation.

However, let's be clear here. When people start making statements like "*I prayed that the Holy Spirit would teach me,*" one must stop to ask how the Holy Spirit could *possibly* be teaching *three* or *four* different versions of the *same* theological topic. Each person who holds a different view than another individual (who also prayed that the Holy Spirit teach them) believes he or she is correct in *their* view and that the Holy Spirit taught *them* and taught them *directly*.

Logic demands that not all of the various views can be correct, therefore the Holy Spirit could not have taught each of the opposing views as truth. Yet, to each their own - and their own views are correct. I have been guilty of making statements similar to this as well, thinking that the position I came to hold was due to the teaching of the Holy Spirit. A number of years later, I discovered new evidence which gave me a new understanding of that same doctrine and caused me to *modify* my view.

Here are examples of the dogmatism that comes with believing that your view and your view only was revealed to you by the Holy Spirit:

"There is no PreTribulation Rapture. Mark it down. It is not in the Bible."

"The PreTribulation Rapture has no basis in Scripture. It is a myth."

"There is nothing in the Bible that even remotely teaches a PreTribulation Rapture. Period."

Here is My Factual Take on the Subject
No need to continue. You get the idea. What is troubling is when people have determined beyond doubt that issues which are peripheral to salvation are either correct or incorrect. Had these

opinions (that is what they are) been stated with disclaimers like "*In my opinion...*" or "*It seems to me...*" or "*I believe...*" or something else along those lines, they would be easier to accept and deal with.

However, when people toss out declarative statements like the ones above, they are designed to stop all conversation that opposes it. In fact, the person who makes these hard and fast statements obviously has no wish to discuss the possibility that they may actually be incorrect in *their* view. In their mind, they have been "taught by the Holy Spirit," and because of this they **believe** wholeheartedly that the Holy Spirit has helped them arrive at certain conclusions. It is unthinkable that they could be wrong. They are the authority on that particular subject. Since they believe this to be the case, then for them the discussion is *closed*. There is no room (or need) for debate, because they are convinced that they are 110% correct.

In studying any theological topic, it should be obvious that it is extremely important to *thoroughly* search the Scriptures - and folks, as you are aware, in most cases this takes a great deal of time, depending upon the depth of the particular topic being studied. Eschatology is difficult at best. Most of us should know this, and it takes merely a glance into Daniel to know how much Daniel studied the writings of the prophet Jeremiah. This is the same Daniel who prayed three times each day, and the same Daniel who was greatly favored by God. It is clear that Daniel wanted to know God's will, and it is also clear that he dedicated himself to two things: 1) *prayer*, and 2) *studying*.

Daniel was Incorrect!
It is also remarkable to note - *and this is very important* – that Daniel arrived at certain conclusions based on *prayer* and *study*. Unfortunately, it turns out that his timeline was *incorrect*. What? How could Daniel have been incorrect? After all, he studied and prayed diligently to know God's mind, and he arrived at an *answer*! How could he have been wrong? Well, as it turns out, he *was* wrong, but

he was also *humble*. When Gabriel indicated that Daniel was wrong, he was quickly able to switch gears, humbly receiving this new information. In other words, he was *teachable*. Let's read the text.

"In the first year of Darius the son of Ahasuerus, of the seed of the Medes, which was made king over the realm of the Chaldeans; In the first year of his reign I Daniel understood by books the number of the years, whereof the word of the LORD came to Jeremiah the prophet, that he would accomplish seventy years in the desolations of Jerusalem." (Daniel 9:1-2 KJV).

Wasn't Daniel a Man of Prayer?
Here we see that Daniel has probably spent a good deal of time studying and praying regarding the prophet Jeremiah's book. Because of this, Daniel arrives at a conclusion, which he believes is correct: that the years of Israel's captivity were almost over - 70 years. All right, so far, so good.

"And I set my face unto the Lord God, to seek by prayer and supplications, with fasting, and sackcloth, and ashes," (Daniel 9:3 KJV).

Daniel has just finished studying and believes that he has found the answer for which he had been searching regarding the end of Israel's Babylonian captivity. What does he do? He does NOT issue declarative statements as if he has "arrived" at the truth and others have not. He immediately *humbles* himself before the Lord, by seeking Him in prayer and supplication. He also fasted, put on sackcloth, and put ashes on his head. Obviously, if someone is going to spend time doing that, we are talking about a length of time. It is clear then that he prayed and fasted for a period. We are not told how long. It could have been one day or seven days. However, it was during Daniel's prayer of thanksgiving, confession, and request that the angel Gabriel appears with the answer to Daniel's prayer. Please note, though, that Daniel was in the middle of confessing HIS sins as well as the sins of Israel when Gabriel interrupted him. He was not cavalier in his attitude toward sin or God's holiness.

Gabriel Offers the Truth

Gabriel then reports to Daniel that it is *not* 70 years, but 70 *sevens* of years (cf. 9:24), or "seventy weeks"! In one fell swoop Daniel goes from thinking the time of captivity is almost over to realizing that it is *not* 70 years, but 490 years, which means it is nowhere near over! The next chapter shows us Daniel's grief and sorrow over this news. In fact, verse two states that Daniel had been in mourning for three weeks (21 days)! That is a long time to be in mourning, but then again, the news he had received from Gabriel had not been at all encouraging. Notice, though, that in Daniel 10:1 it says, "*In the third year of Cyrus king of Persia a thing was revealed unto Daniel, whose name was called Belteshazzar; and the thing was true, but the time appointed was long: and* **he understood the thing, and had understanding of the vision**," (emphasis added; KJV)

Daniel Was Teachable

<u>Now</u> Daniel actually understood the message, whereas *before* he only *thought* he understood it. If anyone thought he was being guided by God's Spirit it would have been Daniel, who prayed three times daily and kept himself as pure as possible. He arrived at a conclusion based on his study, his way of life and his prayer and supplication to God. Yet it was *wrong*, ultimately receiving correction. Had you asked Daniel if he was *sure* about the 70 years (as opposed to the 490 years) he might have told you that he was *quite sure*! Yet he needed to be *corrected*.

My point is simple: ALL of us need to approach the Lord's Word in humility. Even *after* we arrive at certain conclusions, we need to be willing to acknowledge that we *might* be incorrect in our view. This does *not* mean that we become indecisive Christians, unable to show why we believe as we do. It means that we develop a *teachable* spirit, understanding that we will never arrive at perfect knowledge in this life. It just will not happen, as much as we would like it to. We need to have a teachable spirit within us, which only comes by learning in humility before the Lord. Proverbs 15 states, *"He that refuseth instruction despiseth his own soul: but he that heareth reproof getteth understanding. The fear of the LORD is the instruction of wisdom; and before honour is humility,"* (Proverbs 15:32-33).

Eschatology Should NOT be a Fightin' Word

Too many Christians have turned aspects of Eschatology into fighting words. Words are used as weapons to defeat anyone who deigns to disagree with us. *"How dare he disagree with me! Isn't he aware that I have been taught by the Holy Spirit?!"* What about humility? How can we express love to the brethren if we are ready to "kill" them with anger-filled words of rebuke?

In my opinion, the only views worth fighting for are those that are directly or indirectly connected to the following:

1. The Deity of our Lord Jesus Christ (John 1:1; John 20:28; Hebrews 1:8-9).
2. The Virgin Birth (Isaiah 7:14; Matthew 1:23; Luke 1:27).
3. The Blood Atonement (Acts 20:28; Romans 3:25, 5:9; Ephesians 1:7; Hebrews 9:12-14).
4. The Bodily Resurrection (Luke 24:36-46; 1 Corinthians 15:1-4, 15:14-15).
5. The inerrancy of the scriptures themselves (Psalms 12:6-7; Romans 15:4; 2 Timothy 3:16-17; 2 Peter 1:20).

Compared to the above theological areas, how important is Eschatology? Is it something for which you would be willing to die? Are you so sure of your particular belief regarding the Rapture, the Tribulation, the Second Coming, etc., that you are willing to lay your life on the line?

Why did Christians experience persecution and death during Paul's day? Why are Christians *still* killed throughout the world *today*? Is it because they are unwilling to recant their belief in some aspect of *Eschatology*? Hardly. They are killed because they are unwilling to deny Jesus Christ, Savior, Lord and God.

Who is Deceived?
In spite of this, Christians still get caught up in believing that if someone has a wrong view of Eschatology they are in danger of going off the deep end spiritually, even to the point of *losing* their salvation. Frankly, I am much more concerned about people who tell me unequivocally that the Holy Spirit taught them. That makes me nervous. This is not to say that the Holy Spirit does not teach, as I firmly believe He does. However, as I have stated, those who stand behind that use it as a means of *negating* any other viewpoint that is not in harmony with theirs.

It reminds me of the years I spent in the Charismatic movement. All too often, people played the "The Lord told me to tell you" card. Imagine if you ignored that. They would assume that you were in *rebellion*, because the Lord gave them a "word" for *you*, and you were rejecting it. It becomes ridiculous after a while.

Part of the problem within Christendom is not that the Holy Spirit does not teach us. The problem is that we have developed an arrogant attitude that makes us believe that the Lord is *required* to teach us *first* or *directly* about some theological tidbit or position. What about those whom God has actually raised up to *pastor* and *teach* those within the Church? It is understood that they are not going to be 100% correct about *everything*, and neither are you (or me), but that should not preclude our ability to trust their teaching.

God Gave Some to Be Prophets and Teachers…
There are very intelligent, godly individuals whom God has raised up as experts in Hebrew and Greek. There are others specifically gifted

in areas of history or archaeology as it applies to the Bible and the cultures of the Bible. Other individuals are blessed with the gift of applying Scripture to our daily lives. To ignore these people (if they are on target theologically – the five fundamentals) is nothing more than rank *arrogance,* and the Church needs to be done with that.

Jesus warned us that in these latter days there would be many false Christs who would come presenting "another" Gospel. Well, they are here and they have been here for some time now. To the authentic Christian who understands what the Bible teaches about the five fundamentals of the faith (*especially* salvation), these false Christs are obvious. They are presenting *another* gospel and pointing to *another* Jesus. Understanding who they are along with the error they preach and teach keeps us away from them. It normally does little good to debate them.

Theological Areas of Wiggle Room
However, there are also numerous areas of theology in which some wiggle room exists. Eschatology is one of those places. For me, reading a book by a Preterist on the End Times is like reading a comedy of errors. I personally believe that Preterists and the Covenant or Reformed theologian are completely wrong when it comes to the End Times equation. However, they *can* be authentic Christians. There are other areas that contain wiggle room, such as water baptism. Some argue that one must be fully immersed. Others argue that sprinkling fulfills our requirement to obey our Lord.

There are many other topics that we can touch on, like the sign gifts, including speaking in tongues. Are these gifts for today, or did they die out after the last living apostle died? Speaking of apostles, there are those who believe that people can be *apostles* today, and I do not mean merely "one who is sent." I am talking about people who believe they have the same authority as the original apostles. Other individuals believe that those during Christ's time (including Paul) were the only official apostles, ever.

The Great Commission and Eschatology
The Church needs to focus on the thing it was called to do: *evangelize the world.* This is the Great Commission, which Jesus gave to His followers as their marching orders. Yes, Jesus stated that the Kingdom of God is at hand, and what He meant by that was that He – as King – was there (in His day) and His Kingdom was surely coming. It is important to realize that it should be good enough for people to know that one day they either will die or be Raptured, though in either case, they will stand before God. Will they stand before Him at the Bema Judgment Seat (for *believers*), or the Great White Throne Judgment (for *unbelievers*)? The decision each person makes in *this life* regarding the issue of salvation will provide the answer to that question. Views of Eschatology are not part of salvation.

People need to know that they do *not* live forever, nor is their own death far off. It could occur at any moment, and therefore, death is 100% *imminent*, all the time. There is no way to deny or get around that fact, like some attempt to do with their arguments against a PreTrib Rapture.

Go ahead; argue that the word *imminent* does not really mean that the event in question could occur at any moment, with nothing preceding it. Go ahead and apply that to your understanding of the Rapture. However, when you try to apply the same reasoning to the *fact* of your upcoming and *imminent* death, it falls apart.

Death or Rapture
When we all stand before Jesus, what will separate us from those who are lost is one thing and one thing only: *salvation.* My salvation is not affected in any way if my belief in the End Times includes believing in a PreTrib Rapture. In fact, for all those individuals who strongly believe that I am wrong and that my belief could mean ultimately being deceived, I am still waiting for an answer on *why* the fact that my death could occur at any moment does not create within me the *same type of deception or error.*

In other words, people deny the PreTrib Rapture for many reasons; many of them simply man-made. One of the chief reasons has to do with the belief that those who accept as true a PreTrib Rapture will not only be shocked and disappointed when the Rapture does *not* occur prior to the Tribulation (if alive at that time), but they will have done nothing to mature in Christ. Because they believe they will be whisked away instantly off the face of the earth prior to any real drama starting, they have *no* reason to grow (it is claimed).

Apparently, here I sit, twiddling my thumbs as I look to my departure from this earth in the Rapture, which will occur in the twinkling of an eye. Obviously, I cannot be actually *dedicated* to Jesus, desiring above all things to serve Him, because I am simply biding my time as I wait to escape the future horror that this earth will undergo. This position *precludes* spiritual growth and maturity because there is no motivation to follow Christ in service. That is the charge.

Is Today Your Last?
However, am I not supposed to live each day as if it were my last? Could I not die tonight in my sleep, tomorrow in a car accident, or at some point during the day sitting at my desk, composing another blog, or writing another book? The answer is, *of course I could die*, and the appointed time of my upcoming death is unknown to me. I do not know when it will occur, nor can I access that information from God. He is *not* telling, and I am grateful for that. I may realize my death is upon me only mere seconds prior to actual death.

Therefore, if I am to live every day as my last – which is no different than expecting the Rapture to happen any day now – then someone needs to tell me the difference in these two scenarios. In each case, I am:

- *living each day as if it is my last day on earth*
- *living my life submitted to His will, not mine, as best as I can*

- *living with the expectancy of seeing my God, my Lord and my Savior in the next second*
- *concerned about eternal things, not earthly endeavors*
- *separating myself from those things which have no eternal significance whatsoever*

For those individuals who are so sure that the Holy Spirit has taught them that the PreTrib Rapture is wrong, let me ask you this: *Are YOU doing the bulleted list above?* If not, why not? Your death is just as close to you as mine is to me, merely one breath away...always.

No one lives that bulleted list perfectly. No one will in this life, in spite of his or her claims to the contrary. However, if I believe that I could be in His actual presence in any upcoming second, do you think for a moment that this truth causes me sit around filling my face with food, becoming one with my couch while watching my favorite TV show? How absurd is it to think that *this* is what I am spending my time doing, yet this is *exactly* what *anti*-PreTrib Rapturists believe to be true about me and state as if it is fact!

Imminency of Death: No Greater Motivator
Think about something – those of you who firmly believe that the Rapture is far off (at least seven years, at the end of the Tribulation), what is your motivation to live as if every day is your last? You apparently believe that since the Rapture (or the catching away as Jesus returns in His Second Coming) is at least seven years away, there is no reason to think in terms of *imminency*. Every once in a while you may turn your thoughts to death and being instantly ushered into Jesus' presence, but for the most part you are too focused on what you need to do now and how much time you have to accomplish it.

You are forgetting that your death is but one heartbeat away - *all the time.* You are so intent upon dismissing and proving incorrect the belief in the PreTrib Rapture that you have lost focus on living with *imminency*. You spend hours going over your word studies and the Scripture in an attempt to negate any semblance of imminency when discussing Christ's physical return that you have completely forgotten the fact that *everything about life is surrounded in constant, imminent death*!

Everything about our life is *imminent*. Do you need proof of that? You have probably already thought of the same Scripture passages that came to my mind, from the book of James:

"Go to now, ye that say, To day or to morrow we will go into such a city, and continue there a year, and buy and sell, and get gain: Whereas ye know not what shall be on the morrow. For what is your life? It is even a vapour, that appeareth for a little time, and then vanisheth away. For that ye ought to say, If the Lord will, we shall live, and do this, or that. But now ye rejoice in your boastings: all such rejoicing is evil," (James 4:13-16 KJV).

Correct me if I am wrong, but it definitely appears as though James is speaking of *imminency* here and he is connecting it with our deaths. Death will take every one of us, though some will be translated without seeing death. Can we count on the latter? Of course not. It is far safer (and more biblical) to count on the fact that we *will* die.

Your death as a Christian will bring you to the same place that the *Rapture* will bring you to – standing before Jesus Christ at the Bema Judgment. If you are truly living your life as though you could die in the next second, then you are living your life no differently than the authentic Christian who believes that the Rapture will take him or her out of here in the next second, prior to the Tribulation. In either case, the thought of standing before Christ is enough to make your bowels loosen, and that is **not** being stated sacrilegiously. Think about it. In any one upcoming second, you and I could be transported into His presence – through either death or Rapture – and the thought of it *should* at once make us both jump for joy and cause us to *examine* our lives in deep humility and even fear. The people who *never* think about their deaths, or believe that they have at least seven years to go before they see Him, have *far less* motivation to do what I have just described *today and every day.*

Imminency
Do you think – possibly – that one of the reasons Jesus, Paul and others mentioned *imminency* so much is to remind us that our lives are nothing but vapors, in which we are here one moment, and gone the next? Is it *possible* that imminency is just that – *imminent*? Is it possible that we are to learn to come to grips and live with the fact that any approaching second in our lives may be the second that ushers us from this life to the next?

Far from being deceived or straying into areas of erroneous doctrine, belief in the PreTrib Rapture actually causes me to consider (daily) the fact that at any moment I could find myself standing before Him. Will I be embarrassed? Will I wish I had done things differently? I am sure of it, because there is no way I will ever arrive at perfection in this life and in this sin-laden body. The thought that I may see Him in the next instance tends to purify all that is within me, causing me to separate myself from those things which are *worthless*.

Eschatology SHOULD Purify…
"Beloved, now are we the sons of God, and it doth not yet appear what we shall be: but we know that, when he shall appear, we shall be like him; for we shall see him as he is. And every man that hath this hope in him purifieth himself, even as he is pure," (1 John 3:2-3 KJV).

John is saying that when we physically see Jesus, we will instantly become *like* Him. As we dwell on this upcoming change – going from corruptible to incorruptible – purification takes place within us. Our thinking and outlook becomes purified because our mind is no longer dwelling on those things here on the earth, which will all pass away. Because we have shifted our focus to Jesus and the change that will occur in us when we see Him, we then possess the correct mental position to carefully weigh what is truly important in this life: spreading the salvation message, and communicating the salvation that Christ purchased for us, to a lost and dying world. We can be no good as evangelists if we are concerned with life down *here*, focusing on what we have or do not have or how much time we believe we have before we are taken out of this world into His presence. Our focus needs to be spent on knowing that our life here is extremely short (and we've all heard or even said that statement), and the more we understand and believe that, the more our minds will become *like* His.

One day, at a precise moment in time, God will call each one of us home. It will be either through the *Rapture* or through our *death*. Are we living as if each day is our *last*? Proving a point about a particular pet theology is one thing. Living for Christ on a daily basis is another thing altogether. Which one do you find to be more *important*?

Chapter 3
What Is Paul Saying?

If you are one who believes and espouses the PreTrib Rapture position and you have *not* yet been directly accused of being lazy and unspiritual, or even in danger of losing your salvation, consider yourself fortunate. However, it probably will not be long before those accusations are directed your way.

The truth of the matter, though, has more to do with *perceptions* based on *false conclusions* than anything else. Does this particular claim have any weight to it, or have people arrived at this position simply because they *believe* Dave MacPherson has personally proven that the PreTrib Rapture is born of deceit?

This book is *not* designed to address many of MacPherson's charges and claims, primarily because they have been more than sufficiently addressed by others since his first book was published in the early 70s and it has made little difference. Beyond this, it does not really matter what Dave MacPherson *believes*. What this book is designed to accomplish is to at least cause people to *think* about what *they* believe about the PreTrib Rapture and whether or not it is beneficial to label those of us who do believe in it as *deceived* and *deluded*.

In the end, it would be best to understand that if those same reasons for believing that Pretribulationalism results in deceived and deluded individuals are applied to your (and my) *imminent death*, the bottom falls out of the charge highlighted in this chapter, as well as most the other charges directed at Pretribulationalism.

Take Comfort in the Coming Tribulation?
In essence, while the PreTrib Rapture position is often maligned as a "comfort doctrine," the truth of the matter is that it *is* that *because* the Scriptures tell us to rejoice in this fact. Paul mentions in 2 Thessalonians 2:17 that we are to *comfort our hearts* with the information he has just provided. It is certainly difficult to be comforted knowing that you will face the Tribulation period. It makes more sense to understand Paul's teaching to be telling believers that they will *miss* the upcoming Tribulation via the Rapture and *that* is the reason they should find comfort.

Some will argue that the question from the Thessalonians was concerning those who had fallen asleep. Those alive were worried that because some had fallen asleep (which is another way of saying that they had died, since this phrase is *never* used of unbelievers), they somehow missed "the day of Christ" (cf. 2 Thessalonians 2:2b). The Posttribber comes along and says that this reference to the "day of the Christ" refers to the exact day (and only that day) when Jesus Christ physically returns in His Second Coming, at the conclusion of the Tribulation.

If that is true, then why on earth would Paul tell them to *comfort* one another? In other words, if this is the correct understanding, then Paul is stating that those Christians who are alive when the Tribulation occurs will go *through* it, but at the end of it, the dead in Christ will be raised first and then we who are still alive. So, according to this view, Paul is stating that believers will go through the Tribulation and may make it all the way through until Christ's return.

Notice also that the Thessalonians were *confused*, which is why they asked the question in the first place. Had the Day of the Lord already occurred yet? They needed to know. What is going on? Paul assures them that the day had *not occurred*. Paul begins verse two with the words, *"That ye be not soon shaken in mind, or be troubled, neither by spirit, nor by word, nor by letter as from us, as that the day of Christ is at hand."* For most Posttribulationalists, the phrase "the day of the Lord" references the *exact single day* when Jesus actually returns.

If we go with this version, though, the concern of the Thessalonians does *not* make sense. Some Posttribbers get around this by stating that the *error* of the Thessalonians was that they believed the Lord's return to be *imminent*. Actually, I do not see any error in the Thessalonians' beliefs. They were *not sure*, so they asked Paul (via Timothy) for *clarification*. It is more correct to say that the Thessalonians were *concerned* or slightly *confused*, not that they believed *error*. Paul took the time to clarify for them.

How Long is "the day of the Lord"?
It seems clear enough from the text that the Thessalonians had received a letter stating that the day of the Lord had *already* happened. If Paul had already spent time teaching the Thessalonians about the end of the age, with the Tribulation leading to the culminating return of Christ, it is understandable why the Thessalonians became confused. However, it is *only* understandable if Paul is teaching a Rapture *before* the Tribulation. It is absolutely

Eschatology Shouldn't Be a Fightin' Word!

Paul's Meaning in 2 Thessalonians 2

If Paul meant that the "day of the Lord" was the actual single day Jesus physically returns to earth at the end of the Tribulation, then it would look like this:

POSTTRIBULATION VIEW

Start of Tribulation

Second Coming
"day of the Lord" (single day)

- Apostasy
- Man of sin
  - *revealed to the world when he signs covenant with Israel*

Seven Year Tribulation Period

(The worst period in the history of humanity)

Rapture

Start of Tribulation — End of Tribulation

If the above scenario is correct, Paul is attempting to comfort the Thessalonian believers knowing that they will go through the horrors of the Tribulation period.

If Paul meant that the "day of the Lord" was a period of time culminating with the physical return of Jesus at the end of the Tribulation, then it would look like this:

PRETRIBULATION VIEW

Rapture to occur any time prior to Tribulation

"the day of the Lord"
(Culminates in the Second Coming)

Second Coming

- Apostasy
- Man of sin
  - *revealed to the world when he signs covenant with Israel*

Seven Year Tribulation Period

(The worst period in the history of humanity)

Start of Tribulation — End of Tribulation

If the above scenario is correct, Paul is comforting the Thessalonian believers knowing that they will NOT go through the horrors of the Tribulation period.

©2010 F. DERUVO

not understandable if Paul was teaching a Rapture at the *end* of the Tribulation unless the Thessalonian believers were complete morons. If the "day of the Lord" had *already* occurred, would they *not* have already seen Jesus return? Many Posttribbers understand this day as one, single day, as mentioned. If this were truly what it means, then according to Jesus in Matthew 24, every eye would see Him return, correct (unless you allegorize the passage like Preterists do to mean He already returned *spiritually* in A.D. 70)? If the Second Coming *had* already taken place, then the Thessalonians would have *seen* it, pure and simple. The fact that they were asking Paul about it must mean that the "day of the Lord" does not merely incorporate one, single day, but a period of time.

If Paul had *already* spent time with them as he states, *instructing* them about the End Times and the events involved in it, how then could they make such a *huge* mistake concerning the Lord's physical return *if* the Tribulation was supposed to occur prior to it? The contents of verse three makes this clear: *"Let no man deceive you by any means: for that day shall not come, except there come a falling away first, and that man of sin be revealed, the son of perdition; Who opposeth and exalteth himself above all that is called God, or that is worshipped; so that he as God sitteth in the temple of God, shewing himself that he is God."*

Paul's description of the Antichrist is *not* pretty. Paul describes him as being:

- *lawless*
- *a destroyer (like his father, Satan)*
- *one who opposes God and exalts himself AS God*
- *one who openly rebels against the One, True God and demands people worship him instead*

If we consider the character of the times when the above bulleted list is happening on earth, it will obviously not be a pleasant time at all.

One would even be prompted to ask, "How could anyone *miss* it?" How would it be *possible* to miss seeing the Antichrist who exalts himself above all others and demands that people worship him? Unless you're on a deserted island, it would be impossible.

Piece of Cake!
This alone provides a reason in *favor* of a PreTrib Rapture position, and this is what Paul must have already taught them. The believers in Thessalonica were concerned that the day of the Lord had already occurred. If (as the Posttribulationalist states) this (one) day occurs in His return at the very end of the Tribulation, then how would it have been possible for the Thessalonians to miss everything that happened *prior* to that event and the event of the Lord's return as well? In fact, if they *had* missed it, then the Tribulation is obviously a piece of cake to handle! However, Christ's words in the Matthew 24 speak otherwise.

The Thessalonians *must* have been referring to the Rapture *prior* to the *start* of the Tribulation period. This makes more sense, because if the PreTrib Rapturist is correct, then no signs would occur prior to the Rapture, which might be taken to signal that upcoming event. In that case, it would be possible for someone to send a letter stating that this event had already occurred, resulting in the concern for those who had died. Paul assures them that those who had died had not missed the event at all, because the Rapture was still in front of them and the dead in Christ would participate in it as well as the living. He then further clarifies by telling them that those who had died would rise *first*, immediately followed by those who are alive.

Get Your Checklist
If we look at the day of the Lord as a *length of time* which in the Old Testament is normally associated with God's *wrath*, then it *immediately* comes into focus. The Posttribulationalist believes that the Rapture occurs at the *end* of the Tribulation with Christ's Second Coming. Obviously, then, there will be many things that happen

before that event can occur. In fact, if the Rapture does *not* occur until the end of the Tribulation, Christians would actually be able to keep track of the timing of the Tribulation by keeping track of events to know exactly *where* they are in it.

Paul begins verse three with the words, *"Let no one in any way deceive you."* He then explains that the day of the Lord cannot begin until the apostasy *and* the revealing of the man of sin both occur. If the day of the Lord references the *entire* Tribulation period, then it makes perfect sense that that period of time cannot begin unless *two* things happen:

- *the apostasy*
- *the man of sin is revealed*

It is as if Paul is telling them, *"Remember, the Tribulation cannot begin until the apostasy occurs and then the man of sin is revealed to the world. At that point, the Tribulation can begin."* Please also note that in verse 1 of chapter 2, Paul refers to the *"coming of our Lord Jesus Christ and our gathering together to Him."* The question from the Thessalonians appears to have to do with the Christian being *gathered* together *to* the Lord. In verse 2, Paul then refers to the "day of the Lord" as if it is a *different* thing altogether. It does not appear as though he is combining the events.

What is Meant by "Revealed"?
By the way, when Paul speaks of the man of sin being *revealed*, he is not necessarily referring to the event that occurs in the *middle* of the Tribulation. The Antichrist will be revealed when he enters into the seven-year covenant with Israel, and that is the event that signals the start of the Tribulation. THEN the "day of the Lord" can begin as well. The entire world will be watching when the Antichrist (the "who") finally brokers peace in the Middle East. No one up to that point will have been successful. When Antichrist accomplishes it, you can bet the entire world will notice. Thus, he is *revealed*.

Just because Paul *describes* what the Antichrist does *later* (by breaking the covenant and setting himself up in the Temple to be worshiped), it does not mean Paul is equating the event that occurs in the middle of the Tribulation with the Antichrist being revealed to the world. The Antichrist is *revealed* to the world when he enters into a *covenant* with Israel. That will be a showstopper.

The "day of the Lord" is the most recent event that Paul refers to, and *then* tells the Thessalonians *that* day (the day of the Lord) cannot occur until the apostasy and the man of sin is revealed. The Thessalonians asked about the Christian being gathered together with the Lord, and Paul used the *beginning* of the day of the Lord as His reference point. He is ultimately stating, "*Do not worry, because as I told you, the day of the Lord will not <u>begin</u> until there has been a major apostasy and the revealing of the man of sin. Since these events have <u>not</u> occurred, there is no way that anyone has missed the event in which we are gathered together to the Lord.*"

The Bottom Line
Not only is there *nothing* in the text that suggests that Christians would go through the Tribulation, but there is a great deal in the text which shows that they will *not* go through it. To summarize, the question asked by the Thessalonians has to do with whether or not the day of the Lord had occurred. Had it? Could they have missed it? They obviously cannot be referring to the day of the Lord if the day of the Lord means *the end* of the Tribulation when Jesus returns, due to all the *events* and *activity* that would transpire during the time of the Tribulation. It would be *impossible* to miss those, not to mention the fact that if the phrase "the day of the Lord" really refers to Jesus' physical return *only*, would they have really needed to ask that question? Certainly not. Would they not have *seen* Jesus as He destroyed the Antichrist? Would they not have been raptured at that point (if the Posttribulationalist is correct and the Rapture occurs at the *end* of the Tribulation)?

It seems as though common sense dictates that something is wrong with the Posttribulational opinion at this point. It simply does not fit…unless all the Thessalonians were either extremely gullible or complete morons. I believe they were neither.

Would *you* have to ask whether Jesus had returned if the phrase "the day of the Lord" refers to the physical Second Coming? Would you *really* have to ask?

Chapter 4
God is Not Strong Enough?

"I expect the belief in a pretribulation rapture, part of dispensational eschatology, will cause a great apostasy from the faith (2 Thess. 2:3) before Jesus comes again. Believers who find themselves in that awful time of trouble will think that God broke his promise of rapture and they will give up their faith."[1]

The above quote was taken from a website in which the author – *Pastor John* – spends a good amount of time dealing with what he considers to be the heresy of Pretribulationalism. The sad part is that while he began his argument against the PreTrib Rapture congenially enough, it was not long before he allowed his *emotions* to get in the way and do his speaking for him.

---

[1] http://www.clearerview.org/view/?pageID=139274

Pastor John's quote references what many people *believe* to be true about those of us who espouse a PreTrib Rapture. It is thier insistent belief that when the going gets tough, PreTribbers will run from problems as fast as our legs can carry us, moving as far away from God as possible in the process, since we will believe that He has lied to us.

Pastor John's man-made argument is simply untrue. In fact, when I look at the lives of the PreTrib Rapturists I know, I see people who *trust* God, who *serve* Him, who *love* Him and the brethren, and are *learning* to rejoice in difficulties. This is all part of the growth that occurs for Christians, and it is the *sanctification* process that we go through, which Paul speaks about in Romans 6, for starters.

What Pastor John believes is that Dispensationalism (and therefore the PreTrib Rapture position) is *heresy*. He *believes* it to be heresy because of the results that *he believes* will take place within PreTribbers once the Tribulation begins. Note how he equates the PreTrib Rapture with the great falling away that Paul speaks of in his second letter to the Thessalonians. Pastor John simply *assumes* that because *he believes* Dispensationalism to be heresy, then this must of necessity be part of the End Times falling away. This is the routine way of looking at the PreTrib Rapture for many who do *not* believe it to be a biblically defined position.

But What's the Context, Pastor John?
However, if we look closely and honestly within the *context* of Paul's comments to the Thessalonians, we see that Paul mentions this great falling away in the *framework* of the coming "man of sin," (cf. 2 Thessalonians 2:3). Paul states that the falling away *must* occur *before* the man of sin is *revealed*. Pastor John firmly believes this falling away - or apostasy - has to do with the *alleged* heresy of Dispensationalism (of which the PreTrib Rapture is part). My first question is, *where* does he get this idea? Is it because he *believes* the PreTrib Rapture to be wrong?

There is absolutely *nothing* that I can see within the context of this chapter in Thessalonians which would point to a time when people will fall away *because* of their alleged letdown due to the possibility that the PreTrib Rapture does *not* occur as they thought it would. If we take the time to look *closely* at the chapter, we learn something specific does lead people away from the Christ. In fact, this *something* ushers in the man of sin. However, is it related to *Eschatology*? Let's find out.

What *Causes* the Falling Away?
If we consider the verses following verse 3, we see that *something* has in fact occurred *within* society that sets up the perfect introduction for the man of sin (whom most believe to be the Antichrist). What is it that acts as a prelude to his revealing? As listed below, the Antichrist is able to do much, according to Paul. The results of Antichrist's work *builds* upon what people are already *like*. He will:

- Verse 9:
    - *Be in accord with the activity of Satan*
    - *Have all power*
    - *Perform signs and wonders*
- Verse 10:
    - *Create all deception and wickedness (FOR THOSE WHO PERISH)*
- Verse 11:
    - *Be part of the delusion God sends in order that people will accept the Antichrist, and which*
    - *Enables the godless to believe THE lie*
- Verse 12:
    - *These people took pleasure in wickedness, and*
    - *Will be judged*

In looking through that list, I do not see *anything* that even *remotely* indicates that the people who fall away are *believers,* or that this falling away comes *after* the revelation of the Antichrist. In fact, if we consider what Paul has said here, it appears that he is referring to individuals who are *already LOST*. He seems to be describing the tenor of the times in which the period prior to the Tribulation is defined.

Our Friend John Has it Out of Order

Pastor John's exact quote again is (in part): *"I expect the belief in a pretribulation rapture, part of dispensational eschatology,* **will cause a great apostasy** *from the faith…"* (emphasis added)

Pastor John believes he proves his case by adding, *"Believers* **who find themselves in that awful time of trouble** *will think that God broke his promise of rapture* **and they will give up their faith***."* (emphasis added)

If we consider carefully what Pastor John is saying, it is clear that he is providing us with his *belief* regarding *the chronological order* in which the stated events will occur:

1. *PreTrib Rapturists go along expecting the Rapture to occur prior to the Tribulation.*
2. *The Antichrist is* **revealed***.*
3. *The Tribulation begins.*
4. *PreTrib Rapturists are dumbfounded that the Rapture did not occur.*
5. *Now inside the Tribulation, without the Rapture having happened,* **they lose faith***.*
6. *This triggers the* **Great Apostasy***.*

Pastor John relates the order of events as being: 1) the *revelation of Antichrist,* 2) *PreTrib Rapturists lose faith,* then 3) *the apostasy.* But isn't there a problem with Pastor John's understanding of the order of events? Pastor John would only *possibly* be correct if his definition of "day of the Lord" refers to one, single day, which we have already discussed and, I believe, have shown cannot merely be one single day but must incorporate *more* than one day. Here is what Paul says in the same passage that John used:

*"Let no man deceive you by any means: for that day shall not come, except there come a falling away **first**, and that man of sin be revealed, the son of perdition…"* (2 Thessalonians 2:3; KJV; emphasis added).

If we look at Paul's words carefully, *he* states the following will happen, in order of their occurrence:

1. A falling away <u>first</u>
2. The man of sin is then <u>revealed</u>

In Pastor John's scenario, though, he clearly implies that the falling away of believers *comes **after*** the man of sin is revealed. We can assume this because we will only know the Tribulation has begun by seeing the actual revelation of the Antichrist. It is apparent, then, that Pastor John believes the falling away will come *after* the Antichrist is revealed to the world, even though Paul provides a reverse order from Pastor John. Pastor John sees this (which is actually his error) and concludes that PreTrib Rapturists will completely lose faith, which in turn will create *the* falling away or an *apostasy* from the faith.

In another section of one of Pastor John's articles he states, *"Some wrongly call the Great Tribulation the Wrath of God. If that were so, it would mean that God will kill His own people. Who is it who really wants to kill both Jew and Christian? It is the beast, the antichrist. 'And it was given unto him to make war with the saints, and to overcome them: and power was given him over all kindreds, and tongues, and nations.' Rev. 13:7 Satan will sponsor the beast. The Great Tribulation will be the time when Satan will try to totally destroy God's people. The saints are told not to fight back at that time.*"[2] In Pastor John's mind, the Tribulation is the 42-month period when Antichrist wars against the saints. To him, that is when the Tribulation begins and he equates the "revealing" of the Antichrist with the middle of the Tribulation. I see the revealing occurring at the beginning of the Tribulation when he enters into a covenant with Israel (according to Daniel 9:27). In the Daniel 9:27 verse, we are told that "he" enters into a covenant with the many for one week. This is the final or 70th week of Daniel's vision. It is the covenant that Antichrist brokers with Israel that begins the Tribulation, the final week. It is there that the Antichrist is revealed to the world. No one will miss that event, as all eyes have been on the Middle East for years. Even as I write this, the jostling and jockeying for position in the Middle East continues, with no one getting anywhere. When the Antichrist succeeds where others have failed, *that* event will be there for the entire world to *see* and *celebrate*. In my opinion, Pastor John is way off the mark here.

Pastor John is also incorrect about God killing His own people. Satan is *allowed* to kill, but who ultimately controls that? When Babylon or the Assyrians or anyone else was *allowed* to override Israel, slaughter them and/or capture them as slaves, who *allowed* that and often *directed it*? God did. It is splitting hairs to say that God did not direct or ordain Satan's campaign against Job or anyone else. Because God chooses to *use* Satan or the Antichrist does not mean that He is not in control of the situation.

Who Should We Believe?
The apostle Paul lists the events one way, with the falling away occurring first and the revealing of the Antichrist second, but Pastor John reverses them, with the revealing of t he Antichrist *followed* by the falling away. He describes the Beast (Antichrist) who is allowed to make war against the saints. According to Pastor John, then, it is

---

[2] http://www.clearerview.org/view/?pageID=211553

this act of war against the saints that makes people realize the Tribulation has begun. This results (according to Pastor John) in the *falling away* because PreTribbers will wake up to the fact that the Tribulation began and they are still on the planet. Yet Paul states that the "day of the Lord" cannot occur until there is a falling away *and* the man of sin is revealed. Even if we agree with Pastor John that the Rapture occurs at the end of the Tribulation (which we do not), it is clear from Paul's words that first comes the falling away, *then* the man of sin is revealed.

How can an individual make such a drastically obvious mistake in exegesis? The reason is most likely because Pastor John (and those who think as he does) has come up with any number of *fabricated* reasons to believe the PreTrib Rapture position is wrong, and his reasons *seem* to fit. On close inspection, however, they do *not* fit, and are as different as the night is to the day.

Pastor John is saying that *because* I am a Dispensationalist and a believer in the PreTrib Rapture, I am one who *will likely perish.* It is difficult to come to any other conclusion. Paul, though, seems to be *clearly* describing certain attitudes that will be prevalent *before* the revealing of the man of sin (or Antichrist) and which *lead* to the falling away. Apparently, this Antichrist will be in *accord* with the activity of Satan, and will "wow" the populace of the globe - those who have already fallen away.

"I Am God"
The current landscape is one filled with all manner of *deception.* It is building to a strong climax. The world has been expecting someone to break onto the scene that will solve the world's problems. Though it appears differently depending upon the group we are referring to, the deception now enveloping the globe amounts to the same thing.

It does not matter if we are referring to the New Age movement, Spiritual Formation, Contemplative Prayer, or the Emergent Church as a whole. The end result of all these beliefs and practices is to cause us to believe that we are in some way already *divine*. It is merely a matter of our realizing or actualizing our inner, resident divinity, we are told.

This has been the thrust of the New Age movement for generations. It began by teaching practitioners and adherents to begin to focus *inward* on themselves. Transcendental Meditation was used to help people achieve peace within or as a way to become settled inside. Over time, these same practices became more blatant, and eventually the New Age movement began teaching people that we are already *part* of the divine. In fact, because of that it has become perfectly acceptable to promote your own alleged divinity and godhood. It is no longer considered eccentric to claim to *be* divine.

The New Age movement is nothing more than *the lie* Satan told Eve, who listened and *agreed* with him (thereby calling God a liar when she did so). In other words, Eve believed "what was false" about herself. Eve was *not* god – either with a small "g" or large "g." She was a human being - made in God's image to be sure - but she was not god/God. Yet she *believed* the Tempter when he told her that she was or could be *like God*, and today the New Age movement tells people the very same thing. This is, as Paul would say, *another gospel*, which is no gospel at all.

What the New Age movement does for the world at large, the Emergent Church does for the *professing* Christian community already connected with the visible Church. The many practices native to the Emergent Church are designed to cause people to *think* that in essence, they are their highest authority and they answer to no one else. This occurs because of numerous anti-God principles involved with the Emergent Church movement, principles designed to *overthrow* God's rule in favor of the person ruling his or her own life instead.

Eric Barger, of *Take A Stand! Ministries*, has produced a brochure in which he highlights aspects of the Emergent Church. The brochure, titled, "How to Spot the Emergent Church," succinctly summarizes this growing and dangerous movement.

Eric states that *"To Emergents, Christianity should be*

- *Experience over Reason*
- *Spirituality over Doctrine and Absolutes*
- *Images over Words*
- *Feelings over Truth*
- *Earthly Justice over Salvation*
- *Social Action over Eternity"*[3]

Self-Glorified and Mystified

When all is said and done, it becomes clear that the Emergent Church is nothing but a *religious New Age movement*. What is frightening about this is that those who are involved in it are – in my opinion – being set up to accept a coming world leader who will take them *further* into the downward spiral of New Age mysticism and self-glorification.

Consider the fact that in reading Paul's words in 2 Thessalonians 2, people tend to automatically picture vast numbers of people walking *away* from Christ and leaving the visible Church, as our friend Pastor John seems to believe. This will be evidenced (they believe) by people *leaving* the churches (or the faith) that they have attended for some time. After all, how will anyone *know* that a falling away *has* actually occurred unless it is *seen* by the masses?

It is clear that Satan is obviously smarter than people give him credit for being. Is it possible that Satan is *creating* the falling away (the great apostasy)? Could he be doing this by having people *continue to*

---

[3] Eric Barger, *How to Spot the Emergent Church* (Take A Stand! Ministries, 2009)

attend church, all the while adopting the *New Age doctrine* (read: deception)? I believe that this is *exactly* what he is doing.

Part of the Apostasy? Pastor John Believes So

Our friend Pastor John believes that not only is Dispensationalism *part* of the coming apostasy, but he believes that it will be *the* cause of it ("*I expect the belief in a pretribulation rapture, part of dispensational eschatology, will cause a great apostasy from the faith*" – emphasis added). I do not get this same sense from Paul at all.

In fact, when I read Paul or Peter (they both discuss a falling away), the sense I get is that the heresies they point to *all* have to do with *another gospel* and *another Christ*. Peter states, "*But there were false prophets also among the people, even as there shall be false teachers among you, who privily shall bring in damnable heresies, even* **denying the Lord that bought them***, and bring upon themselves swift destruction,*" (2 Peter 2:1 KJV; emphasis added).

Please notice that in the above text, Peter is saying that the false prophets who indoctrinate people with various heresies do so with *lies* that *deny Jesus as Savior*. In other words, all of the destructive heresies introduced by false teachers *directly* relate to the doctrine of **salvation** (denying the Lord that bought them). Why? Because it is the most important of doctrinal subjects, which tie the deity of Christ, the virgin birth, His vicarious death, His resurrection, and the Trinity in among them. Get these wrong, and you do *not* have salvation!

An Aside

Now, I know people like John Gerstner and others believe that Dispensationalism *is* that other gospel because it allegedly teaches two forms of salvation. This is *not* what Dispensationalism actually espouses.

The reason Gerstner and others believe Dispensationalism teaches two forms of salvation is due to *one* brief comment made by C. I.

Scofield in the publication of the very first version of the Scofield Study System Bible in 1909. Scofield's comment was related to a portion of the gospel of John and it seemed to indicate that grace played a part in salvation but so did *works*. The comment was corrected with the first revision.

Had Gerstner and others spent the time to read *all* of Scofield's articles and comments, they would have had no recourse but to admit that Scofield did *not* believe that salvation was by works and grace in the Old Testament, and grace alone in the New. In spite of this, the charge persists to this day, because we have new people reading Gerstner's words for the first time and they believe him when he accuses Dispensationalism of teaching two methods of salvation.

Who Actually Teaches Two Methods?
Interestingly enough, Covenant Theology actually espouses the two-salvation view. In general, their belief (although this varies) is that for Adam and Eve, salvation was by *works*. All that Adam and Eve had to do was *not* eat of the fruit of the one tree.

This lack of action on their part would have likely assured their eternal life/salvation. Because they *disobeyed* God and gave in to their desire to eat, the resulting *action* (or work) created the fall. With it, the sin nature was created. However, the problem is that salvation has *always* been by faith, which is the absolute *belief* in God's Word – written or spoken.

It is clear that Adam and Eve initially *believed* God because they *avoided* the tree. There came a time, though, when they *chose* to *believe* Satan, and in doing so stopped believing God, which led to open rebellion. In other words, it was their *lack of faith* (or the fact that they discontinued believing God) which was their sin and caused them to display that sin *outwardly*. The outward *action* of sinning was a natural result of switching their allegiance *to* Satan.

Yet the Covenant Theologian says that for Adam and Eve, their salvation had to be *earned* through the *work* of avoiding the tree that was off limits. After the fall, Covenant Theology tells us that from that point onward, everyone's salvation was received through *faith*. It is my contention that Adam and Eve sinned the *second* they chose to believe Satan. The outward physical act of eating the fruit stemmed from their *inner* sin, as prelude to their outward act.

Dispensationalism states that *everyone's* salvation has *always* been by faith, *including* Adam's and Eve's. The ceremonial works that those within the nation of Israel were required to keep were done because that was simply the way God mandated that He was to be approached. Those ceremonial acts or works had *nothing* to do with salvation. Salvation for Israel was always by faith. It is *faith* that allows God to credit a person's account with righteousness. Works has nothing to do with it; never has and never will.

And We're Back!
Getting back to the situation at hand, the apostle Peter also speaks of the latter days, or End Times, and his picture is not pretty. He states: *"Knowing this first, that there shall come in the last days scoffers, walking after their own lusts, And saying, Where is the promise of his coming? for since the fathers fell asleep, all things continue as they were from the beginning of the creation. For this they willingly are ignorant of, that by the word of God the heavens were of old, and the earth standing out of the water and in the water: Whereby the world that then was, being overflowed with water, perished: But the heavens and the earth, which are now, by the same word are kept in store, reserved unto fire against the day of judgment and perdition of ungodly men. But, beloved, be not ignorant of this one thing, that one day is with the Lord as a thousand years, and a thousand years as one day. The Lord is not slack concerning his promise, as some men count slackness; but is longsuffering to us-ward, not willing that any should perish, but that all should come to repentance,"* (2 Peter 3:3-9; KJV).

In looking at Peter's words, we *should* get the picture of our society...*today*. Are there people alive today who are *mocking* the return of Jesus? Do these *same* people and many others follow after their own lusts? Yes, they do. In other words, people will be *self-centered*, pandering after their own desires in an effort to make themselves more comfortable in this life. They will *mock* what God has done and what God in Christ has stated about His own return. They will not put up with the five fundamentals, or the orthodox beliefs of the faith, preferring instead to chase after illusions found within the Emergent Church or New Age movement.

Ex-Christians and Their Reasons for Leaving the Faith
I wrote a book a few years back titled *The Anti-Supernatural Bias of Ex-Christians (and other important topics)*. In it, I cited many of the beliefs that I had personally learned of regarding why people who called themselves Christians eventually left the faith. Many of these individuals spent years in the church, praying, singing hymns, tithing, and doing things that they believe represented them as Christians. Eventually, though, one by one these same individuals wound up leaving the faith entirely. Many of these alleged ex-Christians (an oxymoron to be sure) today are either agnostics or outright atheists.

In all my research, not one time did I ever come across someone who left the faith due to reasons related to Eschatology. It was not even remotely a part of why they left Christianity. These folks left the faith for all sorts of reasons, many of which were highlighted in my book, but not once that I could find did *any* of their reasons have to do with the End Times. Not once.

Yet, to hear many people - like Pastor John - tell it, Dispensationalism with its resultant PreTrib Rapture position is *the* problem. According to him, those who believe that the PreTrib Rapture will occur are the ones who will supposedly leave the church, rejecting Jesus when they realize that the PreTrib Rapture has not occurred while the Tribulation has begun. This is in spite of the fact that all around us people are *physically* leaving Christianity and *rejecting* the one, true God, while others *remain* in church but reject Him and embrace the teachings of the Emergent Church.

Simply put, Pastor John apparently does not see what is happening in the church *today*. He does not see and understand that there are many within the setting of the *visible* church who are *currently* leaving it and *rejecting* God, though continuing to *attend* church. Is he unable to notice that there are multitudes that remain in church but simply switch allegiances to *another* (Emergent) church, which caters to the idea that all of us are *divine*? In some cases, the people remain where they are while their church moves toward the Emergent. This has occurred in two churches we have previously attended, forcing us to look for another church each time. Pastor John does not see this (he at least does not mention it), yet the tenets of the Emergent Church teach *another gospel*, which, as Paul would say, is not a Gospel at all. Instead, Pastor John believes that the cause of the apostasy is Dispensationalism/PreTrib Rapturism. In Pastor John's narrowmindedness, he is completely missing the problem.

The "Falling Away" has Nothing to do with Eschatology
The problem is that the coming apostasy and the great falling away is *here now*. It has been here and it is a growing phenomenon that has absolutely *nothing* to do with Eschatology at all. While Satan looks as though he has changed his modus operandi, it is clear that his methods have absolutely *not at all changed*. He has simply become more *efficient* at it.

Satan would like all human beings to believe that we are gods. This is – I believe – <u>the lie</u> that Paul speaks of in his letter to the Thessalonians. How is it possible that Dispensationalism can produce that? It *cannot* do that at all, because of the *orthodoxy* associated with it. Neither Dispensationalism nor the PreTrib Rapture position teaches that we are gods, nor does either one provide a means of arriving at that conclusion or of *rejecting* Him, in spite of what Pastor John and other anti-PreTrib Rapturists believe. In *no* sense does Dispensationalism or the PreTrib Rapture preach *another* Jesus. Salvation is by *grace* alone, through *faith* alone, in *Christ* alone. Always has been and always will be.

Nevertheless, as we have seen, Paul references a coming man of sin who will display an *unequaled* talent for *signs* and *wonders* that this world will gobble up! His works will be in accord with Satan's *current* activity.

What is Satan's *main* activity now? The same thing it has always been, to cause people to believe they are *gods*. If he can fool people into thinking they are gods, they will believe they do not need the one true God! The signs and wonders that will be done by the Antichrist will not only cause people to follow after him, but they will come to believe (through his teaching and example) that they themselves will also be able to do some of those very same wonders. The more people become firmly established in New Age mysticism, the more they will be able to replicate some of these signs on a much smaller scale. Demons are standing by, waiting for the opportunity to indwell and/or control more and more individuals - and it *will* happen. People will think they have arrived.

Supernatural Arena of Wonders
This is also what is happening in the Emergent Church. Through things like Contemplative Prayer, Spiritual Formation, Labyrinths and more, people are being indoctrinated into a supernatural arena that is *counterfeit*, which acts as a *substitute* for a relationship with God through authentic salvation. This salvation has been made available only through Jesus and no other.

Through participation in this *supernatural arena of wonders*, people have been and will continue to be more and more deceived by the signs and wonders they *experience*, *see*, or *hear* about. Certainly, these signs and wonders are not as elaborate by comparison to those the Antichrist will demonstrate.

It is *because* people are being led astray to follow their own lusts (just as Adam and Eve did) that they are *embracing* the New Age movement outright, or the New Age movement that has taken up residence (and is growing exponentially) within the Emergent Church. It is plain to see for anyone who is looking, but many people see none of it because they are too convinced that the PreTrib Rapture is *the* ultimate cause for the apostasy.

Paul's Description Does Not Involve Eschatology

Paul again references the topic of the End Times, or Last Days, in his correspondence to Timothy in 2 Timothy 3, when he states, *"This know also, that in the last days perilous times shall come. For men shall be lovers of their own selves, covetous, boasters, proud, blasphemers, disobedient to parents, unthankful, unholy, Without natural affection, trucebreakers, false accusers, incontinent, fierce, despisers of those that are good, Traitors, heady, highminded, lovers of pleasures more than lovers of God; Having a form of godliness, but denying the power thereof: from such turn away,"* (2 Timothy 3:1-5 KJV).

I am trying to figure out how Pastor John reconciles Paul's description with that of PreTrib Rapturists. I do not see how it can be done, unless he is stating that PreTrib Rapturists are in actuality:

- *Lovers of themselves*
- *Lovers of money*
- *Boastful*
- *Arrogant*
- *Revilers*
- *Disobedient to parents*
- *Ungrateful*
- *Unholy*
- *Unloving*
- *Irreconcilable*
- *Malicious gossips*
- *Without self-control*
- *Brutal*
- *Haters of good*
- *Treacherous*
- *Reckless*

- *Conceited*
- *Lovers of pleasure, rather than of God*
- *Holding a form of godliness and denying its power*

If Pastor John or anyone is saying all that, it makes quite an indictment! What I understand Paul to be saying is that these descriptions will be seen in the types of non-religious *and* religious people ("holding a form of godliness...") that will exist in the End Times, though the religious people are not necessarily Christian. These people who inwardly love themselves also love *money*, love *fame*, love what they think they can become, and will fall prey to the lure of the New Age Movement/Emergent Church movements and the mysticism embedded within them. Frankly, I see this happening all around me *now*. Do you? It is as clear as daylight and it is growing worse by the day.

In reference to the PreTrib Rapture, Pastor John also states, "*Will any harm come to those who believe the theory of a rapture before the Great Tribulation? Yes. I expect that belief will help to cause the apostasy of 2 Thes. 2:3 (ESV) 'Let no one deceive you in any way. For that day will not come, [the day of the parousia of Jesus, see v, 1] unless the rebellion comes first, and the man of lawlessness is revealed, the son of destruction ....'*

This word rebellion translates the Greek word apostasia, meaning apostasy, defection, revolt. When people who profess faith in Jesus find themselves in the Great Tribulation, they will assume that God has failed to keep His promise of a rapture, and they will leave the faith. If believers lose their faith, the preachers who today teach false doctrine will have a heavy burden of guilt to carry."[4]

Pastor John's Major Jump to a Conclusion
Unfortunately, I believe Pastor John is terribly *misinformed*. He

---
[4] http://www.clearerview.org/view/?pageID=139274

seems to have also made some sweeping *generalizations* stemming from a complete straw man argument, which is based solely on his *opinion*, not Scripture.

Do you see the jump he has made? He is claiming that those who believe the PreTrib Rapture will be going along through life, fully expecting the Rapture to occur *prior* to the start of the Tribulation. When the Tribulation *does* begin, and PreTrib Rapturists are still here, this will be such a huge disappointment that falling away from God will be the natural result.

The tragedy of what Pastor John is stating is that he believes my faith is nothing but a *shallow*, empty *shell*. He is charging that those who are Dispensationalists and those who believe the PreTrib Rapture position are so spiritually *dead* that there will be nothing there to help us overcome the alleged *grand disappointment* we will experience when we realize that God has "lied" to us.

The fact that this type of judgmental statement is made at all is sad, but the fact that Pastor John and others believe it to be the truth without having proven it from Scripture is even sadder, and smacks of arrogance.

My life is *not* free from trials or tribulations *now* and it *never* has been. As I look back on my life and I remember some very difficult times as a young Christian, I know the only way I made it through those times was due to the Lord and my faith (which was not that strong then) *in Him*. I would like to think that I have grown in my faith and in my relationship to the Lord. Yet this realization is a two-edged sword, because in seeing that I *have* grown over the years, it has also wakened me to the fact that I realize just how far from perfect I truly am!

In understanding this, though, do I give up? Do I hang my head in shame or abject refusal to continue to believe God? No, because I know that if the Lord got me to *this point*, He is capable of getting me safely to Him in the end. Is this not what Peter means when he says, *"But the God of all grace, who hath called us unto his eternal glory by Christ Jesus, after that ye have suffered a while, make you perfect, stablish, strengthen, settle you,"* (1 Peter 5:10 KJV)?

We are told in many ways in Scripture that the persecutions and trials we undergo as Christians are done so that our faith in Him might be perfected. In other words, as the Lord either sends many *tests* my way directly or allows Satan to *tempt* or *persecute* me, the purpose is to break down my reliance upon myself and look to *Him*, the *Author* and *Perfector* of my faith. You cannot be an authentic Christian without experiencing trials of the faith. It is *impossible*.

Who is Stronger, My Spirit or the Holy Spirit?

Is God, through the Holy Spirit, living in me or not? If He is living *in* me, did the Holy Spirit also *seal* me unto the day of redemption or not (cf. Ephesians 4:30)? What does it mean to be sealed by the Holy Spirit unto the day of redemption? Doesn't it mean that *I am sealed unto the day of redemption?* Yet according to our friend Pastor John, I guess I am *not* sealed. I have apparently been kidding myself. Either that or I can somehow break this sovereign seal and lose my salvation.

I can see how I have grown over the years, and the situations that have *caused* me grow. There have been some very difficult times, and I'm sure most Christians can relate to this. God is good though, because through all of that, He and He alone is the One who has kept me from denying Him. He and He alone has kept me on the straight and narrow path, albeit I have received bumps and bruises due to my own efforts and lack of humility at times. But all of this has been for *His* glory and *my* growth.

Regarding the Tribulation, I say *bring it on*! In God's strength, I will be ready for it - *if* I happen to be wrong about the PreTrib Rapture position. Oh, how I long to see Him, but I know that I will not go home one second sooner than He has preplanned me to arrive.

In truth, how absurd it is to believe that though God saves us, keeps us, empowers us, seals us, perfects us, and rewards us, those who believe in a PreTrib Rapture will be so affected with the realization that it did not occur (if that is the way it happens) that the thought of going into the Tribulation will devastate them. I cannot even wrap my brain around the fact that someone thinks like that, yet there it is. What of God's *power*, His *faithfulness*, His love, His *saving* ability?

God's Wrath

As expected, Pastor John also has difficulties with referring to the entire Tribulation period as God's wrath. He says, *"The pseudo-scholarship that teaches a pretribulation coming makes various mistakes. They commonly call the Great Tribulation the "wrath of God." Would God be killing these Tribulation martyrs? No, Satan would. It is not the time of the wrath of God, but of Satan. The wrath of God will begin around Rev. chapter 15."*[5]

Revelation 15 is a fairly short chapter, with verse eight concluding it. The chapter describes the marvelous sight in heaven as a sign to the nations. Here is the entire chapter:

"1And I saw another sign in heaven, great and marvellous, seven angels having the seven last plagues; for in them is filled up the wrath of God.

2And I saw as it were a sea of glass mingled with fire: and them that had gotten the victory over the beast, and over his image, and over his mark, and over the number of his name, stand on the sea of glass, having the harps of God.

---

[5] http://www.clearerview.org/view/?pageID=139274

3And they sing the song of Moses the servant of God, and the song of the Lamb, saying, Great and marvellous are thy works, Lord God Almighty; just and true are thy ways, thou King of saints.

4Who shall not fear thee, O Lord, and glorify thy name? for thou only art holy: for all nations shall come and worship before thee; for thy judgments are made manifest.

5And after that I looked, and, behold, the temple of the tabernacle of the testimony in heaven was opened:

6And the seven angels came out of the temple, having the seven plagues, clothed in pure and white linen, and having their breasts girded with golden girdles.

7And one of the four beasts gave unto the seven angels seven golden vials full of the wrath of God, who liveth for ever and ever.

8And the temple was filled with smoke from the glory of God, and from his power; and no man was able to enter into the temple, till the seven plagues of the seven angels were fulfilled," (Revelation 15:1-8; KJV).

I've gone ahead and left the reference numbers in for each verse to make it easier for the reader to follow along with my comments. If we consider verse one, it is apparent that Pastor John gains his opinion of God's wrath beginning here because of the phrase *"for in them is filled up the wrath of God."* However, it is also clear that **Revelation 6** speaks of the *wrath of the Lamb*, and we will get to that in a moment.

Essentially, what we learn in Revelation 15:1 is that these seven *final* plagues are *also* poured out and represent God's wrath. It does not necessarily mean that God's wrath *begins* here. In fact, it seems clear enough that this is merely introducing the *final* aspect of God's wrath.

Verse 2 is obviously looking toward the time *after* the last plague has been poured out and God has physically taken the victory over the beast. Even though we know *now* that Satan is defeated, for all practical purposes the carrying out of the actual sentencing of his defeat occurs when he is thrown into the Lake of Fire.

Revelation 15 is a *summary* of things, and beginning in Revelation 16, these seven angels pour out the vials of judgment on the earth, which are God's wrath. In Revelation chapters 16, 17, and 18 we read of Babylon being overthrown by God's judgment.

If one considers the fact that the Tribulation itself does not begin, nor does any part of it occur, without God's *direction*, then it takes on new meaning - or *should*. In the most recent quote, Pastor John believes that God would not be killing the Tribulation martyrs, but that that task lies with Satan.

Consider the death of Jesus: God's wrath was poured out on Him for a short period of time *while* He was hanging on the cross, dying. The brutal beating He received, the crown of thorns, and being nailed to the cross was all *God's* doing! This had been decided by the Godhead in eternity past. While Satan was *allowed* to carry out the sentence, it does not mean that he has free reign to do whatever he would like to do and that God Himself is divorced from the picture.

Why *can't* God be the one who is killing the Tribulation saints? Does John mean that though every hair on our heads are numbered and all of our days are appointed by God, when it comes to our physical death, that is left in the hands of Satan? No, the time and the method of my death have been predetermined by God.

So, apparently Satan has more power than God to determine *when* and *how* people will die? The only reason Satan has *any* power at all is that God gave it to him and allows him to continue to have it.

What about all of the times in the Old Testament when God *judged* the nation of Israel? Sometimes He used natural causes, but most often He *used* another nation. God used that nation as an arm of His judgment against the only nation He has ever created; Israel.

In fact, God uses Satan *against* Christians (temptation, trials, persecutions, tribulations) for two purposes: *His glory* and *our growth*. Satan is nothing more than a *pawn*. He is used by God to bring glory to God and He does God's bidding whether he likes it or not. Why would God *not* use Satan as an arm of His wrath and judgment against Israel, as well as the inhabitants of the world who have constantly and consistently rejected Him, during the Tribulation period? Israel is living in rebellion and has been.

Just because there are multitudes of people who come out of the Tribulation with salvation (praise the Lord!), this does not mean that the entire Tribulation period does not represent God's wrath. Obviously, His wrath is *not* wrath when it concerns His own people; nonetheless, the Tribulation period is a time of God's wrath. It is the final attempt by God to make this world stand up and take notice, *on their own, of their own volition*. Many continue to refuse to do so.

It is splitting hairs to say that Satan is the one who pours his *own* wrath out onto the world. Satan has been doing that since the Garden of Eden. However, Satan is completely *controlled* by God. Satan does *nothing* without God's permission. Just ask Job, from the Old Testament book of the same name. In this book, we see one thing occurring; however, this one thing had two sides to it.

1. *Satan poured out HIS wrath on Job to move Job to deny God*
2. *God ALLOWED Satan to pour out his wrath to <u>perfect</u> Job*

In this very same book of Job, it is clear that a tornado wipes out Job's children. It is clear that the tornado *came* from Satan, yet it is equally clear that God *gave* Satan the permission to do that and placed limits on Satan. The way Pastor John speaks, it is as if God literally hands the reins of death over to Satan so that he can do what he will. No, Satan does what he does only by permission from God.

To believe that Satan is given the first part of the Tribulation to do whatever he wants to do is *absurd*. Does God say "*Okay Lucifer, you've got three and a half years to do your worst, and then I'll take over. Let me know when you're done*"? Sorry, this makes absolutely no sense at all, especially given the fact that the entire book of Revelation opens up with Jesus Christ and John's first words are, "*The Revelation of Jesus Christ, which God gave unto him, to shew unto his servants things which must shortly come to pass,*" (Revelation 1:1a KJV).

The plain fact is that *everything* that occurs in the Tribulation is under God's *sovereign direction*. God *uses* Satan, Apollyon, and the hoard of demons from the pit, famines, pestilence, earthquakes, and the like for a number of reasons:

1. To get the world's attention
2. To chastise and perfect Israel
3. To cause unbelievers to turn to Him
    a. To perfect those who DO

Everything that occurs within the confines of the Tribulation is seen from *heaven,* and this is where everything *originates* as well. The first three chapters in the book of Revelation show Jesus speaking directly to the churches through John.

When we arrive at chapter four, John is called up to heaven, where he now sees things from *God's* perspective. Once John is there, he immediately directs our attention to God's throne and the One who sits on it. Notice that surrounding the throne are flashes of light and peals of thunder. This is a *frightening* reality that John faces.

Please note that when we come to chapter 5 of Revelation, the first thing we notice is a *book*, which is in Jesus' hands. This book is sealed with seven seals. As it turns out, only *one* Individual is found worthy to break the seals and open the book, and it is Jesus Christ. The remainder of chapter 5 highlights the worship of Jesus by all in heaven.

As we arrive at chapter 6, notice that Jesus is the One who *breaks* the seals. Immediately after that, one of the living creatures calls the first seal to go out to the earth. It is the *Antichrist*. In quick succession, the next five seals are broken open onto the earth: *war, famine, death, martyrs* and *terror.*

Whose Wrath?

This next part is very important. In chapter 6, beginning with verse 15, we read the words, "*And the kings of the earth, and the great men, and the rich men, and the chief captains, and the mighty men, and every bondman, and every free man, hid themselves in the dens and in the rocks of the mountains; And said to the mountains and rocks, Fall on us, and hide us from the face of him that sitteth on the throne, and **from the wrath of the Lamb**: For **the great day of his wrath is come; and who shall be able to stand**?* (Revelation 6:15-17; KJV; emphasis added).

As far as the people of the earth are concerned, *they* understand these frightening events to be *directly* from the Lamb of God, and they understand them to be evidences of *God's* wrath, not Satan's. Our friend Pastor John does not see this, stating that God's wrath does not begin until Revelation 15.

I am at a loss to understand why he is not able to read these words and understand that the seals here represent God's *wrath*. Obviously, for anyone who is an authentic Christian at this time, what they experience will *not* be God's wrath, even if they experience the *exact* same thing. What they experience will be situations that will *try* them, *mold* them, and *perfect* them, while glorifying God.

As far as the world, and all who are *not* saved, is concerned, this is nothing more than God's wrath being poured out onto a permissive world, which has continued to reject God. It is Jesus Christ who breaks each of the seven seals. He is in total charge of *what* occurs and *when* it occurs. *I do not see Satan in this picture at all, do you?* Satan is not so much as *mentioned* here, because this is all about Jesus Christ. God's time has come. His patience has been exhausted.

In spite of what I have just pointed out, Pastor John has the temerity to call what I have just done *"pseudo-scholarship."* *If* this first part of the Tribulation Satan is pouring out his wrath, why is he not even in the picture? Why is Jesus *directing* everything? Why do the people on the earth *know* that these seals represent the *wrath of God*?

People like Pastor John give Satan far too much credit and power. His power is completely overseen by God Almighty. Satan can do nothing on his own and the only things he *can* do are those allowed by God.

The Antichrist and the Parousia
One final note regarding Pastor John, and then we will move onto another one of the many manmade claims against those of us who believe the PreTrib Rapture to be the "official" view of the Bible. Pastor John makes this statement regarding the Antichrist and the Parousia: *"[Pretribbers] commonly teach that the antichrist will begin his work after the rapture. The rapture occurs at the parousia of Jesus, according to 1 Thess. 4:15. Paul wrote that the antichrist will be destroyed by the parousia of Jesus. 2 Thess. 2:8. If he will be killed at the parousia of Jesus, he cannot begin his work after the parousia, can he?"*[6]

---

[6] http://www.clearerview.org/view/?pageID=139274

We need to take a look at what he is referencing. In order to do this, it would be wise to consider the *entire* context, not just the one verse in 2 Thessalonians 2:8. The verse in question, in its surrounding context says, *"Now we beseech you, brethren, by the coming of our Lord Jesus Christ, and by our gathering together unto him, That ye be not soon shaken in mind, or be troubled, neither by spirit, nor by word, nor by letter as from us, as that the day of Christ is at hand. Let no man deceive you by any means: for that day shall not come, except there come a falling away first, and that man of sin be revealed, the son of perdition; Who opposeth and exalteth himself above all that is called God, or that is worshipped; so that he as God sitteth in the temple of God, shewing himself that he is God.*

Remember ye not, that, when I was yet with you, I told you these things? And now ye know what withholdeth that he might be revealed in his time. For the mystery of iniquity doth already work: only he who now letteth will let, until he be taken out of the way. And then shall that Wicked be revealed, whom the Lord shall consume with the spirit of his mouth, and shall destroy with the brightness of his coming," (2 Thessalonians 2:1-8; KJV).

Pastor John understands Paul to be saying that when Jesus returns, He will destroy the Antichrist. I would *agree* with him. However, John does not see the break in Paul's teaching. Let's face it; if what John is claiming were true, then obviously PreTribbers would have to be complete morons to not see it. The truth, though, is that it is not that easy, as John would have us believe.

As an aside here, while I agree that PreTribbers generally teach that the Antichrist cannot begin his work until after the Rapture, it is more accurate to say that he cannot begin his work *officially* until he enters into a covenant with Israel for seven years. This is very important. Pastor John is assuming that the *Parousia* mentioned in 2 Thessalonians is the same as the Rapture. During the instantaneous PreTrib Rapture, Jesus does not *return physically to earth.* During this time, he steps out of the third heaven to *call* his Bride up. I have created an illustration, which sheds light on this, on the next page.

Paul states that "the coming of our Lord...and our gathering together to Him" cannot occur until:

- *The apostasy occurs*
- *The man of lawlessness is revealed*

After Paul relates these two events, he goes off on a bit of a digression in order to shed more light on the man of sin. It is very much like a *parenthesis*. It would be as if I said something like this to a friend:

"I think after I get home from work tonight, I'm going to cook one of those frozen chicken dinners and then go bowling (you remember last week I was talking about going to go bowling this week since I got my new bowling ball. This will give me more practice time for the upcoming tournament). Anyway, I'm not sure how long I'll bowl, but at least a few hours. Did you want to come with me?"

Paul is literally stating (my paraphrase):

"The Day of the Lord cannot happen unless the apostasy occurs and then the man of sin will be revealed (this is the same man of sin I already told you about who will set himself up as god in the holy place, but will ultimately be destroyed when Jesus returns to the earth). Please remember that even though Satan is working behind the scenes to accomplish his ends now, he will be able to ramp things up once the Restrainer is taken out of the way."

After introducing the man of sin into his teaching, Paul then simply adds more *description* about this man of sin. He is not necessarily stating that all of these things that he describes will happen immediately. He is simply *reminding* the Thessalonians of what he had already taught them (*"Do you not remember that while I was still*

Eschatology Shouldn't Be a Fightin' Word!

with you, I was telling you these things?"). What Paul is doing is nothing more than *digressing*, and people go off the point all the time in conversations, but eventually return to it.

What is amazing is that most of us talk like this in daily conversation, yet Pastor John reads this passage and believes that Paul is speaking chronologically, in quick succession. Actually, whether Pastor John or any other Posttribber can appreciate it or not, Paul could easily be stating that only *one* event (the apostasy) will occur prior to the revealing of the Antichrist. This is the guy who will be destroyed when Jesus *does* return to earth in His Second Coming.

There is nothing in the text that demands it to be understood Pastor John's way. The same could be said of the way I understand it, which is all the more reason that Christians need to stop being so dogmatic about Eschatology! It serves no good purpose to beat other Christians up with words of denigration when it is possible that the Posttribber might be wrong in his interpretation and the Pretribber might also be wrong.

Eschatology Shouldn't Be a Fightin' Word!

Chapter 5

"Make It Stop!"

It is clear that those opposed to the PreTrib Rapture have decided that those of us who believe it to be taught in Scripture are immature, unspiritual and have no real depth as Christians (if we even *are* Christians). That is quite a denunciation if you stop to consider the ramifications of it.

I have to wonder why those who are opposed to the PreTrib Rapture look immediately to any alleged negative ramifications that they believe to be resident within the belief itself. It is very common to hear or read comments like, *"it seems that one of the greatest difficulties for [PreTribbers] (besides just the natural aversion to the idea of having to endure the tribulation!) has to do with confusion about the imminence of Christ's coming."*[7]

If you consider the words quoted above from Steve Hall, it appears as though what is being said is that the belief in the PreTrib Rapture should be discarded because:

1. *It creates an aversion to having to endure the Tribulation*
2. *It is based on a wrong understanding of the doctrine of imminence*

The first reason is a straw man (and an ad hominem attack) and should be discarded. It is completely fabricated. What folks like Hall are doing is *assuming* that PreTrib Rapture folks do not want to go through the Tribulation, so we have *created* the PreTrib Rapture position. This makes little sense if one stops to consider that wishing does *not* create God's will. God creates His will. Because Hall and others do not see the PreTrib Rapture position in Scripture, then they must assume that the reasons for adopting this position have to do with *self-centeredness* and *fear*. This also assumes that there is no biblical merit in the PreTrib Rapture position.

Now, while it is understood that people who are opposed to the PreTrib Rapture position are so because they do not *see* it in Scripture, this does not in and of itself mean that it is actually *not* there. There are people who do not see proof of the deity of Christ or the Trinity in the Bible either. This in no way negates these doctrines.

The second reason listed above only has merit if the individual is correct about his understanding of the word "imminent" and its place in the Second Coming of Christ.

---

[7] http://www.aboundingjoy.com/Bible%20studies/imminency.htm

Is It Pride?

We will deal with imminency shortly, but let's take a minute or two to focus on reason number *one* in more detail. The PreTrib view of the Rapture should *only* be discarded if it is *not* found in the Bible, correct? Hence, no amount of manmade, fabricated or straw man arguments essentially have any merit whatsoever if the position *is* taught in Scripture. The PreTrib Rapture position should *not* be discarded because of fabricated arguments like the alleged aversion to having to endure the suffering of the Tribulation. It really has no bearing on anything.

However, this is the difficulty when people arrive at these shallow, manmade arguments which *they* purpose to be the truth, or at least some type of evidence in support of their viewpoint. Who *said* PreTribbers have an aversion to suffering? Who *said* that because I see the PreTrib Rapture in Scripture, I am wiping the sweat from my forehead because I believe I have obviously dodged a powerful bullet? Who said that because I (allegedly) have no wish to suffer at the hands of the Antichrist, I and others like me grabbed onto the PreTrib Rapture as a solution to the problem? If it is *not* in Scripture, then it is no solution at all! I am only kidding myself if it is not true.

Why does Steve Hall automatically assume that the reason people believe and espouse a PreTrib Rapture position is because we are afraid of persecution, trials, tribulations, and the ultimate seven-year Tribulation? It almost appears as though he came to that conclusion and *then* decided that it must be at least one of the reasons why people such as me espouse the PreTrib Rapture. Let's face it, I'm a huge chicken! Cluck, cluck, cluck!

However, let's take a look at the *reverse* side of this argument. Whether Steve Hall (or anyone else who makes that statement or ones similar to it) sees it this way or not, his comment is *extremely* arrogant, and one that is born of *pride*. I am sorry to say that, but it appears to be true. I realize that for Steve, it is likely just a throwaway remark or an aside, said with a twinkle in the eye. It is actually an insult against all of us who understand the Bible to be teaching a PreTrib Rapture position.

Look at Me! I'm Wonderfully Spiritual!
The implication of his offhand comment is such that it points *back* to Steve and *his* apparent desire to go *through* the Tribulation. It is like someone saying, "*Folks, do you see how spiritual I am? Do you sense my strength, my faith, my trust in the Lord? Do you see how ready and willing I am to die for my Lord? Do you see how wonderful and truly spiritual I am? If not, I will be happy to give you the details by comparing myself with any PreTribber.*"

I am not saying that Mr. Hall *means* his words to come across this way, but this is the unfortunate implication, simply because he seems to have enjoyed pointing out (the *fallacy*) that PreTribbers do *not* want to go through the Tribulation. It has nothing to do with whether we *want* to go through the Tribulation or not.

Steve Hall is implying that *he* is ready, willing, and able to suffer for His Lord, though it seems clear to him that PreTribbers are *not*. Though the PreTrib Rapture might *actually* be taught in the Bible, as far as Hall and countless others are concerned, they are convinced that it is not.

At least one of the reasons the PreTrib position exists is due to the fact that there are those of us who just plain do *not* want to suffer at all, not now, not ever - so there. We won't do it and you can't make us!

It is a classic case of providing a reason against a view that has nothing to do with anything. This reason is certainly not *biblically* based. If the Bible *does* teach a PreTrib Rapture, then the reason for Hall's statement can be seen for what it is: *arrogance*.

Eschatology Shouldn't Be a Fightin' Word!

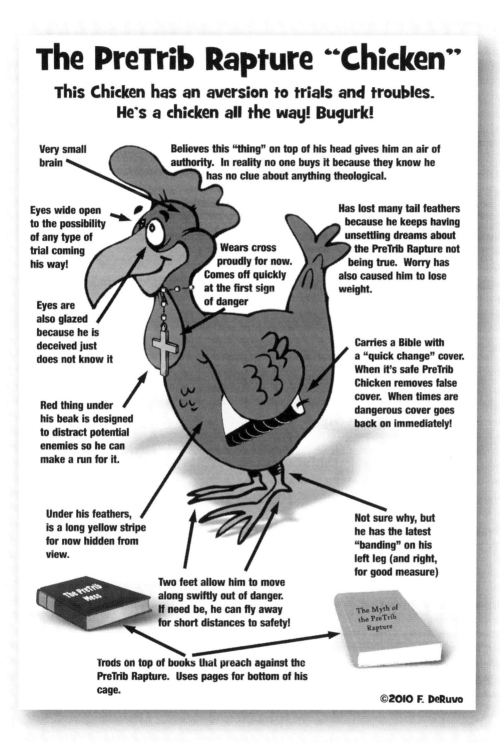

Let us assume, for the sake of argument, that Hall and all those who believe as he does are *correct*. That means that at least one of the reasons I am a PreTribber is that I *am* a chicken. This led me to search the Bible to *find* something that supports my chicken nature, allowing me to breathe a sigh of relief and wipe the pooling sweat from my brow.

Based on this, then, would it not be true that all those who believe that they *are* going to live through the Tribulation (if it occurs on this earth when they are alive) are *not* fearful (or at least, not as fearful of it as I supposedly am)? In other words, Posttribbers should be the most stalwartly unafraid Christians on the face of this earth. They *know* they are going to suffer at the hands of the Antichrist. They *know* that they will be hounded for being a Christian and will suffer persecution for it, to the possible point of *torture and death*.

Is this the *case,* though, with Posttribbers and others who reject the PreTrib Rapture? Is this their real point of view? Well, is it? Inquiring minds would really like to know. One would certainly think it *would* be the case. On the contrary, I have found that it is *not* the case at all! Surprise, surprise!

Chapter 6
I am Not Afraid (Much)!

The most interesting thing I have come across recently in my studies, research, and inquiries, is that *far* from Posttribbers being revved up to suffer for their Lord, they appear to want to *hide* from such a prospect. How do I know this? I have heard it directly from Posttribbers themselves and in emails to me, as well as the fact that I have read things to that extent on their Internet discussion forums. It is a mind-boggler for sure, because on one hand, these folks can condemn, reprimand, and disparage PreTribbers for their alleged fear of suffering; yet on the other hand, they seem unable to see their own fear and how *they* are dealing with it! Just because they believe that *they* will be here during the Tribulation and PreTrib Rapturists do not *want* to be does not make their belief true. The very fact that many of them speak of hiding or building an underground shelter is no different from my alleged aversion to suffering. It looks like they are making other plans to avoid having to standing before the Antichrist.

Not long ago, as I was cruising the 'Net, compiling research for this book, I came across a site with the opening tagline: *The Pre-Trib Rapture is NOT in the Bible.* Unable to contain myself, I took a peak to see what I could see. As far as arguments against the PreTrib Rapture and those in favor of the Posttrib Rapture, there was nothing new. However, I did find one section of the forum interesting. One of the discussion threads was titled *What can we do to prepare ourselves for Tribulation? Should we?* It caught my eye, so I went in for a closer look. Of course, my first question is *Why would anyone who does not believe in the PreTrib Rapture position feel the need to prepare for the Tribulation* (as if preparing for it will actually help)?

Once inside the discussion thread, there were some comments that I found to be very telling. I've listed a few of them that I thought beneficial to share below. They are quoted exactly as they were written on the board. I've made no changes to spelling or grammar or anything else. For that forum's protection, I am deliberately *not* listing the URL, or the full names of those posting the comments.

"I beleive the Bible clearly says we are not to prepare but to let the Holy Spirit take control of (enter) our bodies and speak through us so we can be a perfect example to the non-believers as to bring more souls to the Lord through Christ. I know I should be backing this up with Scripture, but I'm at work now and need to do some research and studying to make sure of my point. Although I do believe we should always be dressed in the full Armour of God, in which case I think we would be prepared for anything." - B

"I agree with you, our primary preparation should be Spiritual. But, I was thinking of Joseph in the Old Testament, God showed him a vision and they were able to prepare for the famine. Do you think there is any thing in that for us?" – R

"Yes I think we should prepare to take care of our families. I have plans for an underground dwelling that will be stocked with water and rice etc. I am only doing it for a hobbie though really as I have full trust in theLord and am not worried in the least of the dreaded 4 horsemen." – B

*"If he feeds the birds, then He'll take care of us. For aren't we more valuable to him than the birds? He said that somewhere...
I don't think that hoarding things and creating a shelter will be that helpful. We cannot assume that we'll still be able to stay where we are or where we keep these things."* – C

"We have no choice but to physically prepare. What will happen when they say you must take the mark to buy/sell? You're only going to have two choices, take it and be doomed, or reject it and run. If you reject it and let them take you, isn't that a form of suicide? Knowing Christians will be killed for not taking the mark doesn't give us the right to surrender. We should live as long as we can to be able to reach more people." – T

"What about the time being shortened? isn't this tribulation not going to be 7 years, but just 5 months? HE does this I beleive because like someone said before, 1/2 the faithful will be decieved (1/2 the virgins). He shortens the time for the sake of the Elect. Because Satan is such a good Impostor that save the shortened time we would all sucumb. That's the time limit I'm basing my "lamp oil" for. not 7 years." – B

"Good point B. We debate in Saturday Shabbat class about how much shorter that time will be. It's a deep subject." – T

"I've never heard of the 5 months of time shortened... Where did it say that? That would so rock if that were to happen!!" – C

"Matt. 24:22. is one i place I know Jesus said the time would be shortened. but somewhere in the O.T. i think it gives the 5 month period. remember when dealing with prophcey from the Bible.. anything expressed in months (months=lunar cycle/night time=darkness) is refering to Satan. and anything expressed in days (solar cycle/day time=The Light) is refering to Jesus, The Light of the World. I'm going to try and bring more references in about the five months of darkness (no quiencidence the same time spent on the ark when you add the 40 days and the time it took the waters to go down)." – B

"Revelation 9 talks about the locusts torturing men for 5 months. They may be getting the 5 months from that. I wouldn't bank on that being the time limit on the tribulation." – R

The previous posts, as I say, were from one particular discussion forum. My heart actually goes out to these folks, because they are simply *guessing* (and some of their guesses are simply terrible). They do not seem to know what to do, in spite of the fact that Jesus said not to worry about tomorrow.

As I continued searching, I came across one website that actually provided a plan for surviving the Tribulation:

1. **"Get yourself right with God**: Repent and turn from every sin in your life and seek God with all your heart.
2. **Get out of debt**: If you don't it will become a snare to you.
3. **Store food, water and other essential supplies**: The World is heading for a Global famine, stocks of wheat and rice are at an all time low and shortages already exist.
4. **Consider moving**: The Cities will be a very bad place to be in during the Tribulation, there will be civil unrest and much

violence and martial law will be implemented in many cities to curve the looting and violence and to control the public.
5. ***Withdraw your cash and move your money***: *The Global credit crunch is bringing the World economic system to its knees with the collapse of the US subprime mortgage market and the banks worldwide struggling to survive due to their liquidity problems and bad investments.*
6. ***Seek God with all your heart and trust Him completely***: *Remember we cannot save ourselves from what is to come, only God is able to see us through the coming Tribulation.*
7. ***Stay watchful and remain faithful***: *Even if things should appear to go quiet, and nothing much appears to be happening, know that this delay is only the calm before the storm.*"[8]

Most websites I found that had anything to do with discussing preparations for the coming Tribulation simply said things like, *"Prepare! Those who do not provide for their families are unfaithful!"* or things similar to this.

I have also run across anti-PreTribbers who have plans (or have begun) to build a large storm cellar type of expansion underneath their home. Others have purchased land in the country and their plans include building a type of underground shelter which will allow them to survive the horrors of the Tribulation period.

The difficulty with all of the suggestions, plans, and scenarios listed is that it is clear that no one *knows* what they should do! But for those who are planning to hide out in an underground shelter, one wonders what the purpose of that is going to be? If we are here to do the Lord's work, then does He actually want us to *hide* from the world?

---

[8] http://www.maranathaweb.com/tribulation_plan.html

Is this an "Aversion," too?
At the same time, isn't *hiding* during the Tribulation the exact same thing as *having an aversion* to being there and possibly suffering? In my mind, while PreTrib Rapturists are accused of not wanting to suffer, Posttribbers apparently do not see the incongruity of their own statements when they say they want to escape the horrors by *hiding* where they will (hopefully) not be found.

If those opposed to the PreTrib Rapture believe that they will go through the Tribulation (provided they are alive when it occurs), then are they not to be doing what they should be doing now, which is *evangelizing the lost* and trusting God on a daily basis? If they are evangelizing the lost *now*, then what effect would hiding underground have on any opportunities to witness? In fact, how are their actions any different from their charges against the PreTrib Rapturist?

The anti-PreTribber believes that I want out of here because I do not want to suffer. It is because I do not want to suffer that I have apparently put together parts of Scripture to create the doctrine of a PreTrib Rapture, so fearful am I of having to go through the Tribulation. I have convinced myself that I will be gone with the rest of the Church before the Tribulation occurs.

But numerous anti-PreTribbers seem to have the same mind. Their plan involves hiding...underground...with a ton of food...lots of water...a generator...plenty of fuel for the generator...and a *cloaking* device, which will shield their position from the authorities.

I'm Hiding – You Can't See Me – Na, Na, Na, Na, Na!
Can someone please tell me what the difference is between the two scenarios, because I do not see it? While someone might say, "*Look, just because Posttribbers attempt to hide and keep themselves and their families safe, it does not mean we won't be found by the Antichrist.*" This response simply begs the question. The truth is that

Posttribbers do *not* want to be found by the Antichrist (at least the ones who have their shovels ready and have begun moving dirt).

Consider, though, that as a PreTribber, I am doing my level best to remind myself daily that this could be *my very last day* on earth. The Lord may call me home. No, I am not referring to the Rapture. I am referring to my *death*.

If I am living with the expectancy of my *imminent* death, then how am I living? Well, hopefully, I am spending the day being aware of how to live my life *for* His glory. This means that I make the most of every opportunity to evangelize. It also means that I treat other people the way Christ would treat them. It means that as I go through my day, I am praying for people – my family, my friends who know the Lord, my friends who do *not* know the Lord, my pastor, my church family, and many others as well – so that the Lord's perfect will may be done in their lives. Not only that, but also that as His will is accomplished in their lives, they will grow (willingly, by submitting) and He will be fully glorified.

If I am living my life as if *today* was my last, do I do the following?

- *Worry about food?*
- *Worry about water?*
- *Worry about clothing?*
- *Worry about unexpected things that may occur in life that I cannot even foresee?*
- *Plan what I'm going to do next year or the year after that without submitting those plans to the Lord?*
- *Waste time with worthless events or activities?*

Before anyone misconstrues the above list, let me clarify by stating that I believe God *does* wish us to supply our family's needs. I also believe that God would have me make intelligent decisions throughout the day as situations arise, and to make those intelligent decisions I will need to trust Him for wisdom.

I further believe that it is fine to look ahead into the future and make *potential* plans, with the proviso that these things will only occur if it is the Lord's will. Finally, knowing that I may be taken at the end of this day causes me to look at life differently, to determine what is actually useful and beneficial for me to be involved in as one of His children and as a servant of the Most High.

Am I going to watch foolish movies that are not beneficial? Will I make good choices about music? Will I do those things, which I know will not embarrass me when I stand before Him?

Global Persecution
A good many missionaries are scattered across the globe who are currently suffering for Christ. They suffer because they are Christians and because they are busy spreading the Gospel of Jesus Christ, often into hostile territory. They have gone into territory that is governed by the lord of the air, Satan himself. He does not like giving up any ground, nor does he give up any humans who serve him, without a fight. Sometimes, that fight includes physical harm to Christians. God allows all of these things. For the saint, it is for growth and the Lord's glory. For the unbeliever, it is the Lord's wrath.

If we consider the book of Daniel, for instance, we see this come into play. Daniel 3 tells us of the courage of Shadrach, Meshach and Abednego. They refused to worship the golden image that Nebuchadnezzar had built in his likeness, or at least an image that represented him and his power. People were to bow down to this image and *"at what time ye hear the sound of the cornet, flute, harp, sackbut, psaltery, dulcimer, and all kinds of musick, ye fall down and worship the golden image that Nebuchadnezzar the king hath set up,"* (Daniel 3:5, KJV). Those who refuse would be thrown into the fiery furnace. We learn from the previous chapter that Daniel had pleased King Nebuchadnezzar when he interpreted his dream for him. The king rewarded Daniel by making "*him ruler over the whole province of Babylon, and chief of the governors over all the wise men of Babylon,*" (Daniel 2:48, KJV). Daniel had also asked that Nebuchadnezzar would allow him to appoint Shadrach, Meshach, and Abednego over the province of Babylon.

In chapter 3, when Nebuchadnezzar had his special golden image constructed and gave the order that all should worship it whenever they heard the music playing, Daniel's three friends refused. For this their punishment was to be thrown in the fiery furnace, and it is interesting to note that the furnace for them was made seven times hotter than usual.

When the three men are brought before Nebuchadnezzar, you have to really appreciate their candor and their unwillingness to give into the king's demands. They essentially told the king that God was absolutely able to save them from the fiery furnace. However, if God chose *not* to do so they would still praise Him, as all their worship went to the one, true God and no one else (cf. Daniel 3:16-18). As you can imagine, Nebuchadnezzar was extremely angry. He did not like being disrespected like this, and because of his anger, he had the furnace prepared and the men tied and thrown in.

God's Wrath
Here is where it gets interesting. Verse 22 of chapter 3 tells us that because the furnace had become so hot, the men who brought Shadrach, Meshach and Abednego *to* the furnace to toss them in were actually killed because of the heat! In my opinion, this is God's wrath in view, which He pours out either on those who rebel against Him (as in Israel) or the unbelievers who continue to believe a lie.

Of course when Shadrach, Meshach and Abednego were tossed unmercifully into the furnace, not only did it not kill them, but they did not even smell like smoke when they came out! Moreover, there was a fourth individual in the fire with them! (cf. Daniel 3:25-27)

Satan intended to inflict harm on Shadrach, Meshach and Abednego and he used his followers (in this case, the Chaldeans of Daniel 3:8) to accuse the Jews. Satan wanted them dead. God would use this situation for their growth and His glory.

In fact, even in the deaths of the men who died bringing Shadrach, Meshach and Abednego to the furnace, God is glorified. Satan is defeated at each turn.

This same principle holds true when Daniel is thrown into the lion's den. God protects him, yet those who accused Daniel in the first place were also tossed into the lion's den and received no such protection. Again Satan attempted to kill someone who belonged to God and was thwarted. God used that event to allow the attempted murder of Daniel to glorify Himself and mature Daniel. When those who had accused Daniel were also thrown into the lion's den (along with their families), God was glorified once more.

Today's Global Missionary
In spite of the tremendous amount of cruelty many of these brothers and sisters in the Lord suffer, this is *not* signaling that the Tribulation has begun, as some think. Their persecutions are being directed at them because they have deliberately obeyed God and gone into enemy territory for the purpose of introducing people to Jesus Christ. The same thing would happen to any of us, and if these persecutions did happen to us, it would only be due to God allowing it for our *growth* and for His *glory*.

One website states this: *"There are some among us teaching there will be no tribulation, that the Christians will be able to escape all this. These are the false teachers that Jesus was warning us to expect in the latter days. Most of them have little knowledge of what is already going on across the world. I have been in countries where the saints are already suffering terrible persecution."*[9]

It is difficult to completely understand what this individual is saying. Is she referring to Preterists and Covenant Theologians who believe that there will be no future Tribulation because (they believe) it occurred in A.D. 70, or is she referring to PreTribbers who believe that there will not be a Tribulation *for the Church*? It could be taken either way, but since I have come across this comment many times in books, articles and websites referring to PreTribbers, taking it to refer to PreTribbers is as logical as taking it to refer to Preterists.

If she *is* referring to PreTribbers, notice how she applies the label "false teachers" to this group? The correlation between saints who are already being persecuted (and have been for decades) and the Tribulation is simply not there. The Tribulation is God's wrath poured out on an unbelieving Israel and an unbelieving world. It is clear that in both cases, multitudes come out of the Tribulation as saved individuals. Amen.

The persecution that exists (and has existed since Christ) is part and parcel of being a Christian. It goes with the territory, but this in and of itself is not God's wrath. It is God allowing Satan to create havoc and situations in which Christians are often martyred for their faith. For that, they receive additional rewards from God.

But if, as the individual above states, the Tribulation is yet coming, and she equates this with persecution, then why weren't the persecutions of Nero or Diocletian or anyone else considered to be the Tribulation? If we are going to use persecution as a proof of the Tribulation, then the Tribulation does not really stand apart. It is simply more of the same, but severely ramped up in brutality and horror. Persecution is not a sign of the Tribulation. Persecution has

---

[9] http://www.arkhaven.org/christian-community.htm

always been around and it will *continue* into the Tribulation period. The thing that makes the Tribulation stand out is the fact that it is God's time to pour His wrath out onto the world and the people living here, both Jew and Gentile. His wrath is clearly seen as early as Revelation 6 and continues from that point on.

The Christian is guaranteed persecution, trials and general tribulations. This is because the world hated Jesus, and this same world will hate us. This still has nothing to do with God's time of wrath. His wrath is designed to get the world's attention, and He has been patient long enough. It is time for God to put the pressure on people so that they begin to feel what it will be like in hell, even while they are still alive.

Nero
It was likely tempting for those apostles and believers who lived during Nero's persecution to believe that the Tribulation had begun. It had not. What *they* experienced was certainly God-ordained, but that persecution does *not* represent *the* Tribulation that Christ spoke of in the Olivet Discourse. Persecutions tend to come in cycles, and a good deal of it depends upon the state of the world. Over all of this is God's guidance.

When *any* Christian is persecuted, put on trial, harassed, or even ultimately killed for their faith, this is *never* God's wrath that has caused it. The Tribulation period will be a time of nothing *but* God's wrath poured out on the earth and its inhabitants. Can God protect those who become saved during that time? Of course, but if they are killed, their death is *not* representative of God's wrath. It is *fallout* from His wrath being poured out on unbelievers and spilling over to the lives of Christians. There are occurrences in Revelation where God does not allow anything to hurt anyone who has God's seal, like with the locusts from the pit, for instance (cf. Revelation 9:5). It is unequivocally clear that God is in full control of all that happens during the full seven years of the Tribulation. There should be no doubt of that.

Only the SECOND Half of the Tribulation is God's Wrath?

The *entirety* of the Tribulation is a period of God's wrath. Just after the midpoint, *after* the Antichrist has set himself up as God, Israel realizes they have been completed duped, and they literally run for the hills. God protects those individuals. In his anger, though, Antichrist nearly bursts a spleen, and he turns his vengeance onto the rest of the populace who belong to God.

Posttribbers and most other anti-PreTribbers like to point out that it is at *this* particular point during the Tribulation that God's wrath begins to pour out. My question is *why* is this said to be God's wrath? In other words, they state that during the *first half* of the Tribulation it is *not* God's wrath that is being poured out onto the earth at all. It is *Satan's* wrath.

However, when we get to the midpoint and we *know* beyond doubt that the Antichrist is out for blood (literally) and he goes on a rampage, this period is then described as a time of *God's wrath*. This makes absolutely no sense.

If anything, the *first* part of the Tribulation should be ascribed to God's wrath with the *second* being ascribed to Satan's (through the Antichrist), yet this is not what anti-PreTribbers believe or teach.

As a PreTribber, I do *not* have a problem with understanding that the entire Tribulation period is perfectly designed by God. In His own time, He will take Israel aside – with an outstretched arm – and *deal* with them. Now, since Israel is in a state of unbelief, then it is His *wrath* that He pours out onto that nation. He also takes the time and opportunity to pour out His wrath on the rest of the unbelieving world, due to their constant and consistent rejection of His rule over them.

Whatever happens to those who turn to Him in faith during the Tribulation, they will experience trials and testing, but *not* His wrath. Since it is clear from numerous places in Scripture that the Church is *already* pure, already clean, and already prepared, there is no need at all for any part of the Church to go through a period in which God's wrath is completely and unrelentingly poured out onto Israel and the world.

If we consider the fact that the instant we see Jesus we will be *like* Him, this should tell us a good deal (cf. 1 John 3:2). Many today say that the Church *needs purification*. How can that be, if the God of heaven (cf. Romans 1-7) already declares me righteous? If I am currently declared (or judged to be) righteous by God Himself, then how is it possible that I still need to be purified?

Granted, I realize the difference between justification and sanctification. I understand that the moment I receive Christ I am declared righteous by God, because Christ's righteousness is credited to my account. That righteousness will never run out and is always efficacious enough to cover every sin I ever commit.

Sanctification, on the other hand, is a process of being set apart, as we know. This sanctification will take place for the remainder of my earthly life, but the very instant I transfer from this life to the next John says that I will be *like Him*. That means that the thief on the cross was like Christ. That means that anyone who has ever experienced an authentic deathbed conversion becomes like Christ as soon as they leave their mortal bodies.

Sanctification is for our growth while we remain here on earth, and it also is the means by which God completes a good portion of His will (through believers). This sanctification produces good works (God's definition of good, not ours). These good works grant us the privilege of receiving *rewards* at the Bema Seat of Christ. Those rewards do *not* make us more pure. They provide additional rewards for the believer.

To say, as many do, that the Bride of Christ needs to be purified is to completely misunderstand justification and the process of sanctification.

If I become a missionary to India because God calls me there, and as part of that work I am persecuted and eventually killed because of my faith, that is part of the trials and tribulations that God decreed for me long ago, before I was born. These have nothing to do with God's wrath which is poured out during the Tribulation. Nothing at all.

Back to the Present

It is impossible to predict what will occur in our lives from one day to the next. The most we can do is *plan*, understanding that all of our plans are waiting for God's approval or disapproval. Those who live each day as if their *last* are motivated to live rightly, doing, saying and thinking the things that bring glory to God. Those who live each day believing that the "end" (or our lives) is near do so to the honor and glory of God. The end of my life is always one breath away, therefore it is always *imminent*. Say what you want about the PreTrib Rapture, but there is no getting around that truth about my imminent death.

The tragedy is that too many people today believe that the PreTrib position is not only wrong, but *heretical*; yet if I die today and have lived this day as *if* it was my last, then I am doing things *correctly*. On the other hand, if I live this day believing it could very well be my last (due to the Rapture), I am somehow a big *chicken*, wanting to escape the persecution of the Tribulation (according to many).

So it appears that in spite of the similarities and even equality between these two events (both causing an end to my physical life on

Eschatology Shouldn't Be a Fightin' Word!

The ENTIRE Tribulation Is God's Wrath

7-Years of Tribulation Signaling the End of God's Patience with Israel and Humanity

*Seven Seals — Seven Trumpets — Seven Bowls

Trib Starts with Israel signing Covenant with Antichrist

Midpoint when Antichrist Breaks the Covenant and Demands worship

Trib Ends when Antichrist is destroyed at the Coming of Jesus Christ!

(*Seals, Trumpets and Bowls All Come from Same Seven-Sealed Book, which is ONLY Opened by Lamb)

6 Reasons Why All of Trib is God's Wrath

Jesus is the Only One Found Worthy to Open the Seven-Sealed Book (Revelation 5)

Tribulation Would Not Begin if Not For the Lamb Opening the Book

Israel Signs Covenant with Antichrist (Daniel 9:27 - 70th Week)

Antichrist is REVEALED to the World

Earth Dwellers Speak of the Wrath of the Lamb (Revelation 6)

Petrified with Fear of LAMB'S wrath!

Satan is NOT in the Picture at the Start of the Tribulation; Only Christ

Tribulation Begins with the Command of Jesus (Revelation 6)

Tribulation Ends with the Return of Jesus (Revelation 19)

©2010 F. DeRuvo

earth), it is only the first one (my death) which is considered the *spiritual* option. The version with the Rapture at the end of the day is apparently *not* causing me to live *for* Christ, but instead I am living *for* myself, instead of God. If this makes sense to you, maybe you can explain it to me, because to date, anti-PreTribbers have not successfully proven their contention with Scripture.

I understand that because the Rapture is believed to occur *prior* to the Tribulation, then the assumption is that it is the Tribulation that is scaring me into *wanting* the Rapture to happen. The focus then is the Tribulation, instead of the Rapture, which would usher me immediately into His Presence.

However, living my life as if it could end *today* is considered spiritual because there is no one horrible event that I am hoping to miss (like the Tribulation). The trouble is that the *anti-PreTribber* is the one who makes this connection, *not* the PreTribber. For the PreTribber, death is death, leaving this earth is leaving this earth. One moment I'm here, the next I'm with my Lord. If given the option by Jesus Himself, which would *you* choose?

Do you really want to stay here forever? Do you actually *want* to be here just to see how bad life can get under the despotic rule of the worst egomaniac since the beginning of time? Do you need more crowns? If it works out like that, it works out like that.

It seems to me, though, that all the Posttribbers I have spoken with believe they will go through the Tribulation as if it is a done deal. That tells me that they are not even considering the fact that they could die long before the Tribulation ever starts. They do not seem to understand what I consider to be their faulty thinking on the matter. They are not thinking about the fact that they may die *today*. They are concentrating on the upcoming Tribulation instead.

For those who believe it is their duty to *want* to stay and experience the hell (literally) of the Tribulation: who are you *kidding*? *Why* do you want to stay here? Do you believe the Lord's will won't be accomplished until and unless you are persecuted for your faith unmercifully and possibly torn limb from limb or beheaded in the process?

Do you believe that God needs to take you and put you through a living nightmare so that you will become *perfected*, fit for His Kingdom? If you believe that, then you have failed to understand your true standing in Jesus Christ as explained by Paul in the first eight chapters of Romans and elsewhere.

You have failed to understand that as members of His Church, His Bride, He has *already* washed us. It does not require martyrdom to accomplish this purification. We have already been washed in the blood of the Lamb, died into His death, and raised again with Him. We are **now** joined to the *Living* Christ if we are authentic Christians, actually having received the salvation that He purchased for us. He has forgiven our sin – past, present, and future – and He has *declared* us righteous. He has *sealed* us with the Holy Spirit until we see Him in the next life.

Chapter 7
Why Not Preterists?

I have always wondered why there is a storm of vitriolic verbiage directed toward the PreTrib Rapturist, yet people who hold other positions are not as attacked. While some Posttribbers do come out against the Preterist position on this or that, or someone will write a book or article on how wrong Amillennialism is for instance, in general people save their worst righteous anger for the subject of the PreTrib Rapture. Why not the other positions? Why not come down on the MidTrib or PreWrath positions of the Rapture with the same amount of vigor? Why not take that same level of indignant anger and address the Preterist or Covenant or Reformed Theologian because of *their* belief that the Tribulation has already occurred? Why is it just the PreTrib Rapture individual who is called:

1. Deceived
2. Deluded
3. Plain Wrong
4. In danger of losing salvation
5. Heretic
6. Part of the Great Falling Away
7. Part of the End Times Apostasy

Try to put your own opinions about the PreTrib Rapture position aside for a moment. Does it not seem strange to you that the above list contains words and phrases that are *liberally* applied to PreTrib Rapturists, but *not* to Preterists or Covenant or Reformed theologians?

Lazy Bones and Spiritual Immaturity
The largest reason why the PreTrib Rapture position is said to be wrong is due to the alleged fact that when the Rapture does *not* occur and the Tribulation begins, all of us PreTrib Rapturists will be standing around with our mouths open. We will awake from the peaceful slumber of our *Tribulation-denial* in which we have been securely cocooned, only to realize that the pit of hell has just been opened. Out of it flies every beast, demon and creature imaginable, which rivals anything seen in any horror movie.

Needless to say, this will *not* be a good thing. Get a mental picture of all of the PreTrib Rapturists standing around screaming, "MOMMY!" because we will realize at that point that we have been duped and are now faced with the reality of the Tribulation. This overwhelming picture of things to come will cause the complete bottom to fall out from underneath the PreTrib Rapturist, so it is claimed. Thus begins the long and quick descent into spiritual oblivion from which the PreTrib Rapturist is said never to return.

Take the Preterist, though, or the Covenant or Reformed theologian. Many to most of them *deny* that there is a Tribulation *yet* to occur. This already happened, they say. It took place in A.D. 70. *That* was the Tribulation. *That* was when Jesus returned (spiritually). Talk to Preterists like Gary DeMar or others who will resolutely tell you that all of it, except for the last few chapters of Revelation, has already occurred. To even *consider* the possibility that the Tribulation is still in front of us is lunacy.

Yet for these people, who deny not just the Rapture, but a seven-year Tribulation, what will *their* reaction be to that reality? I would think it would be on par with the alleged reaction of the PreTrib Rapturist (or worse), who denies that the Church will go through the Tribulation.

If the anti-PreTrib Rapturists' accusations are true *and I* lose faith in God, would not this very same thing be expected to happen with Preterists and those who believe as they believe? In fact, wouldn't it be *worse*? They do not even agree that a Tribulation *will* occur, much less that they will have to go through it (provided the PreTrib Rapture position is wrong). Imagine the shocked look on *their* faces when the Antichrist signs the seven-year covenant with Israel, and voilà! the Tribulation has begun! I can already hear the "uh-ohs."

So I ask again, *why* is the fury poured out *only* on the PreTrib Rapturist? Why do people vent their spleens only on those of us who believe that the Church will be taken prior to the beginning of the Tribulation in what is called the Rapture? Why do not the Preterists and the others share the same fate as the PreTrib Rapturist? It is a puzzle, to be sure. Whoever said people are fair in their thinking doesn't really know people.

Would it not be *fairer* to distribute the indignation flowing from *anti-*PreTrib Rapturists more evenly across the board, as opposed to expending it all only on the PreTrib Rapturist? Why isn't the Preterist considered to be *deluded* or under some major *deception*? Why isn't the Preterist thought to be teaching *heresy*? Why is it mainly the PreTrib Rapturist who is the proud recipient of all the mud pies flung in his direction?

The Devil Makes Them Do It!
There is something terribly wrong with this, which makes me think that since it appears as though *only* the PreTrib Rapturist comes under the constant condemnation of anti-PreTrib Rapturists, maybe there is some truth to it. After all, *if* the PreTrib Rapture *is* the correct position, one of Satan's well known tactics would be to cause people to respond to it in a level *self-righteous anger* that they may not even seem to understand. Is this not the same exact situation case with those who are opposed to Israel and the Jews? The amount and level of anger directed toward Israel *should* make people ask themselves why it is there. Maybe it is the same with the amount and level of antagonism toward the PreTrib Rapture position.

Since many within the ranks of Christendom frequently wield words and phrases like "heretic" and "false teacher" like swords, one can only wonder why the Preterist seems to be left alone. Are *they* teaching false doctrine, or are they not? Are *they* prepared for a coming Tribulation, or will the blood drain from their face as they realize they have *not* wandered onto a movie set filming the latest apocalyptic movie, but have in fact become overwhelmed by the very real, present, and clearly advancing Tribulation?

Chapter 8
Anybody Really Know What Time It Is?

Besides the fact that people are resolutely and determinately *angry* or *frustrated* at PreTrib Rapturists because of the alleged wrong view of the Rapture we hold, there is another problem which comes to the fore. This particular problem is one that, like the *false* notion that PreTrib Rapturists have an aversion to the Tribulation, is also another *assumed* notion by anti-PreTrib Rapture people. Since it is assumed, without Scriptural support, then it is also *manufactured*. This makes it a Straw Man argument. A Straw Man argument is really no argument at all.

There are several realities which exist today concerning the Tribulation. These realities *must* be considered in any discussion of End Times events. Let's assume for the moment that the PreTrib Rapture position is the *correct* position (don't worry, for those of you who are opposed to it. It is merely for the sake of argument). If we understand the PreTrib Rapture position to be the correct position, then the following also falls in line.

1. *If the Tribulation is a Scriptural reality, then it will happen.*
2. *If the PreTrib Rapture is a Scriptural reality, then it will happen and it will also happen prior to the Tribulation, just as its name indicates.*
3. *Though we know the specific event which signals the start of the Tribulation, we do not know when that particular event will occur, giving the Tribulation its official start.*
4. *We do not know when the PreTrib Rapture will occur.*

Given the above information (and remember, we are treating all four points as if they are unqualified *fact*), then we must discuss something else related to the PreTrib Rapture. It is something which seems clear enough that anti-PreTrib Rapturists do not at all consider.

We know that the times are becoming *more* complex, *more* troublesome, *more* chaotic, and *more* in line with what the Bible refers to as the coming age of apostasy. In fact, it should be clear that with the Emergent Church *alone*, apostasy has infiltrated the visible Church in a big way.

What is interesting about this apostasy is that it certainly seems to be occurring *within* the confines of the visible Church, *not* separate from it. All around the United States, as well as other parts of the globe, large churches have popped up literally presenting *another* message of salvation. Whether it is Tony Campolo's take on salvation, or Henry Nouwen, Brian McClaren, Rick Warren, Robert Schuller, Joel

Osteen, or a multitude of other church leaders, they are all guilty of presenting a gospel that has moved outside of the *biblical* definition of salvation. In spite of this, though, there are many within Christendom who seem only to have eyes for the PreTrib Rapturist and Dispensationalist; but I digress.

Anyone who has been awake and paying attention, especially over the past few decades, *should* be aware of a number of things that have changed within our society. These changes have *not* been for the better.

1. **The Anti-Abortion Movement** - has become very pronounced and through their rhetoric has made it much more difficult to protest the taking of innocent unborn lives.
2. **New Age Movement** – has made tremendous gains and inroads into churches, schools, and the lives of people in general.
3. **Public Schools** – have made it more difficult for children to learn by adding more coursework that has little to do with actual learning and more to do with *socializing*.
4. **Homosexuality** – the groups who are part and parcel of the Gay and Lesbian movement have made huge gains in Hollywood and in the public sector. Their virulent attacks on Christians and all who oppose the gay agenda have become more and more the norm. Their goal is that the world sees homosexuality as normal, and they will stop at nothing to see that goal come to fruition.
5. **Socialism** – our government has been making a push toward Socialism for decades, with the Clintons having made great strides. Now, our current President, Obama, has taken the baton and has continued the race with it. Wanting to "share the wealth," he is unapologetic in expecting Americans to sit still as he takes money out of some pockets to give it to others.

6. **Support for Israel** – this has been a hot button issue for years, but with President Obama's obvious refusal and unwillingness to support Israel, he offers a plan of peace that essentially cuts Israel nearly out of the deal altogether. No president before him has taken such an overt stand *against* Israel, but his obvious disdain for that country, along with his support for Islam, is telling.
7. **Assault on Christians** – not necessarily physical here (though that is certainly included in this category throughout the world), but more and more lawsuits are being brought against Christians and Christian churches. One of the most recent examples is the proliferation of lawsuits against churches and the "noise" they make during their worship services.
8. **Terror List** – interestingly enough, for a time the government did not hide the fact that "right-wing extremists" classified as anti-abortionists, those supporting freedom of speech, the right to bear arms, etc., were placed on a "terror watch list."
9. **Physical Violence Against Christians** – is up all over the world. In fact, it has been stated by more than one organization that the total number of Christians put to death in the 20th century is more than all previous centuries before it. Lawsuits, harassments, violence, and more are just the tip of the iceberg.
10. **The Media** – has long been playing favorites, all the while denying that they do. Their favorite game is to deny that they are leftist, while bashing anyone from the right. This has severely ramped up over the past decade and there seems to be no end in sight. What the media refuses to cover is as bad as *how* they cover the news they *do* cover.
11. **UFOs/Alienology** – this is a big one because of the amount of individuals who have stepped forward claiming to have been abducted by aliens. Now, it goes without saying that certainly some of these are fakes; however, even if we take away a

percentage representing that element, there are simply too many with too many specific details to discount. Something is going on in the spiritual realm, and even people who have been studying this area and who are not Christian are concerned.

The above list is merely scratching the surface. In short, unless a person has been living in a cave, it is impossible to miss at least *some* of these areas which have affected our society.

If we add to this the freakishness of nature, the level of severity and frequency of storms, the total destruction these storms leave in their wake and the number of deaths they cause, we are left with a picture of staggering proportions. All of this brings to mind what Jesus speaks of when He described the things that were the beginning of birth pangs in Matthew 24, the Olivet Discourse.

How much worse will things become? Obviously, they can become a great deal worse, and in fact, that would appear to be exactly what Jesus means when He spoke of just how bad things were going to become during the time *prior* to His return to this earth. If you'll take the time to read through Matthew 24 (along with Mark 13 and Luke 21), you'll find that He pulled no punches and stated that this coming apocalyptic time would be the worst time this earth will have ever experienced. Without doubt, we seem to be moving toward that.

The anti-PreTrib Rapturist claims that at least one reason those who believe and espouse the PreTrib Rapture do so because they have an aversion to the coming Tribulation. However, persecution is alive and well on planet earth. There have been periods where it has abated for a time, but in general, it has always been there. It is one of Satan's favored methods of choice. He yearns to bring pain and destruction to Christians in the hopes of getting them to recant their faith. Barring that, it brings a smile to his face if he can just bring them *pain*, and plenty of it.

What About the Time Just Prior to the Tribulation?

The times leading up to the onset of the Tribulation will *not* be like walking through a field of clover, with the birds singing and the breeze gently blowing. The times moving toward the Tribulation – as we have already begun to see – are times which are astounding people. All across the globe, one calamity or another is occurring, and in quick succession. It seems that one barely ends when another occurs.

In the midst of the economic meltdown within the United States and in various places throughout the world, wars and rumors of wars continue. One country postures in the face of another, while the other shows no willingness to back down.

Earthquakes are occurring, with the latest one (as I write this) having taken place in Haiti. Just two weeks prior to that, a 6.5 temblor shook the northern part of California and the southern part of Oregon. Each day, the media brings us more bad news regarding the state of affairs stretching over the entire globe.

In the midst of this, Christians continue to live here as long as the Lord permits, while He takes them home one at a time at the appointed time of their death. Since the Tribulation will only begin at the signing of the seven-year covenant between Israel, the Antichrist, and countries in the Middle East, we simply have no clue *when* that will happen.

Does anyone really believe that it will not get progressively worse as that beginning point draws near? I do not kid myself in thinking that life will go on as before and then all of a sudden, within a day or two, things will go from good to horrible and the gates of hell will open their contents onto the earth.

What I believe *will* happen (and *is*) is that things will *progressively* become worse and worse as they are doing now. There is the great possibility that some grand leader will appear out of the muck of leaders and he will indeed have leadership skills that will amaze people. To be around him will be to know what calm in the middle of the storm really means. He will be a picture of health, vitality, and *outward* integrity. He will be brilliant and will be able to establish himself as a man everyone wants to follow. He will be the Nimrod of the day, promising to fill needs and bring people together as no one has ever done before, and he will be the man of the hour.

In all the commotion, though, things will continue to become worse and worse. A greater measure of civil rights will be removed from everyone, and the ones who suffer the most will be Christians. As it stands right now, President Obama could declare martial law and it might never be rescinded. Think of it: the United States under martial law. Why would any leader of this country who had *declared* martial law ever want to *remove* it?

It Will Only Worsen *While* We Are Here
The whole point being that Christians (yep, even PreTrib Rapture Christians) are *aware* of the fact that even though we believe we will be Raptured *prior* to the beginning of the Tribulation, we really have no clue when that will happen. We cannot look to a particular upcoming point in the future and say, "That's our going home day!" It is simply not the case. Of course, there are those like Harold Camping, who believe they know when Jesus will return, in spite of the fact that Jesus said no one will know the day or the hour. Their guesses do nothing to negate God's plan or His faithfulness. They are going beyond the bounds set by the Lord Himself, and their reward is their own folly. In short, we simply do not know how long it will be before the Tribulation begins. We only know the exact *event* which will set it into motion.

Let's say that as far as God is concerned, the Tribulation will not officially begin for another 15 years, bringing us to A.D. 2025.

If then we have 15 years ahead of us before this event occurs, what is the landscape going to look like *during* those 15 years? By landscape, I mean what will the world's situation be up to and *at that point in time*? If January 2010 is any indication, along with the ability to look *back* to determine just how much things have changed over the past decades, then we can assume without even needing a crystal ball that life in the world will be *worse*, not better.

It does not take a genius to look backwards to see from where we have come. We have all heard the expression "hindsight is 20/20." This is obviously true. It is heard almost as often as "If we do not learn from the past, we are destined to make the same mistakes" (paraphrased from a quote often attributed to philosopher George Santayana). The question, then, is *have we learned anything*? It seems plain that in most cases, we have *not*. Certainly, in the arena of people getting along with people, we seem to have learned nothing at all.

War is *not* a thing of the past. It not only exists, but the machines and technology used in wars are greater in accuracy and greater in potential destruction. Culture clashes exist today, seemingly more than ever before. People's tempers are short, and their ability to lash out at others appears to stem from a greater degree of self-centeredness.

Chapter 9
What Covenant?

Probably one of the most argued definitions relates to God's *wrath*. The Posttribber castigates the PreTribber for believing that God's wrath is the entire period of the Tribulation. The PreTribber argues that the Posttribber does not really understand the meaning of "God's wrath." The MidTribber or PreWrath advocate comes along and says that both the PreTribber and Posttribber are all wet because God's wrath does not actually begin until sometime around the middle of the Tribulation.

The arguments persist from all sides, but it seems to me that something is missing here. It's certainly possible that this has been brought up before, but not to my recollection. Since I have not read every book on the subject, it is very possible and likely that this *has* been stated before, and something is nagging at the back of my mind to that effect. Of the books I *have* read, it seems most likely that Dr. Arnold G. Fruchtenbaum was the one who brought it to my attention through one of his books, *Footsteps of the Messiah*.

At any rate, the very thing that *starts* the Tribulation is *the* reason that God's Wrath begins to pour out from that point onward. In fact, according to Revelation 6, the Lord directs everything from His heavenly throne, including the release of the Antichrist onto the world's scene. However, the fact that the Antichrist may well already be in our midst is not reason enough to believe the Tribulation has begun, or is necessarily close.

Israel Says "Okay" to the Antichrist (e.g. the Devil)
It is the covenant the Antichrist brokers with Israel, along with other countries in the Middle East, which kicks off the Tribulation. Why is this the case? Why is the covenant the green flag for God's wrath to begin pouring out?

Obviously, we are basing our understanding of this covenant on Daniel 9:27. Many people have argued and continue to argue about the meaning of this passage. In fact, many of those arguments have quickly turned into quarrels, quarrels that do not honor God and that keep Christians from involving themselves in the real task at hand, which is evangelism.

I have taken the time to quote from Steve Wohlberg in a previous work of mine titled *A Deceptive Orthodoxy: The End Times "Gospel,"* in which I take issue with *his* understanding of the End Times and what he believes Daniel 9:24-27 teaches. There is no need to repeat it all here, but a brief look at his opinion regarding this 70th week is worthwhile, only because it tends to be in general what most Covenant, Reformed or Preterist theologians believe to be true about this passage.

In his book *Exploding the Israel Deception*, Wohlberg believes that his view of the Daniel passage in question is like dropping a bomb on the entire evangelical world, much like Truman's decision to drop the atomic bomb on Japan. In the former, Wohlberg believes if his view is adopted, the results throughout the evangelical world will be similar to the results of the atomic bomb on Hiroshima. I'm glad Wohlberg is not arrogant about his position.

In Wohlberg's book, as well as another one of his books called *End Times Delusion*, he spends a good amount of time dissecting these four verses in Daniel. He of course comes to a completely different conclusion than most conservative biblical scholars with respect to this view of Eschatology. After quoting Daniel 9:27, he states, "*Have you ever heard of the 'seven-year period of great tribulation'? The whole idea is rooted in two words of the above sentence! The two words are 'one week'. Supposedly, that period of 'one week' applies to a final seven-year period of great tribulation at the end of times.*"[10]

As mentioned, his opinion was thoroughly dealt with in my previous books, so I won't take the time to reiterate it here. Suffice it to say that I point out numerous areas where I believe Wohlberg has made severe interpretive errors.

If the reader has read any of my previous books on the subject, it should come as no surprise that I believe this Daniel passage is extremely clear and forthright, something that Wohlberg denies. In presenting his own view of the passage, it is interesting to see just how convoluted he becomes with his interpretation.

---

[10] Steve Wohlberg *Exploding the Israel Deception* (Endtime Insights, 1998), 42

In Daniel 9:24-27, we learn through the angel Gabriel that Daniel is mistaken in his view that the 70 years of captivity with Babylon were almost up, as written by Jeremiah. In one sense, though the Babylonian captivity was almost up, Gabriel is clearly stating that Daniel's people (the Jews of Israel), will continue to experience some type of captivity from Gentiles for 70 sevens of weeks, or 490 years. The entire context of Gabriel's explanation and the chapter itself when Daniel was attempting to discern the meaning of Jeremiah is *years*. This is why the "weeks" is taken to mean years. As Fruchtenbaum points out, it is almost as though Gabriel was making a pun, or a play on words. "It's not 70 years (sevens), but 70 SEVENS."

We see in the Daniel text that there are clearly 490 years, or 70 weeks, broken down into sections. The four verses state, "*Seventy weeks are determined upon thy people and upon thy holy city, to finish the transgression, and to make an end of sins, and to make reconciliation for iniquity, and to bring in everlasting righteousness, and to seal up the vision and prophecy, and to anoint the most Holy. Know therefore and understand, that from the going forth of the commandment to restore and to build Jerusalem unto the Messiah the Prince shall be seven weeks, and threescore and two weeks: the street shall be built again, and the wall, even in troublous times. And after threescore and two weeks shall Messiah be cut off, but not for himself: and the people of the prince that shall come shall destroy the city and the sanctuary; and the end thereof shall be with a flood, and unto the end of the war desolations are determined. And he shall confirm the covenant with many for one week: and in the midst of the week he shall cause the sacrifice and the oblation to cease, and for the overspreading of abominations he shall make it desolate, even until the consummation, and that determined shall be poured upon the desolate,*" (Daniel 9:24-27, KJV).

Note that Gabriel speaks of 70 weeks, which he breaks down thusly:

- 7 "sevens" or 49 years (7 x 7)
- 62 "sevens" or 434 years (62 x 7)

In the above groupings, there is no break between them. They run concurrently, according to Gabriel. However, at the *end* of the second set of weeks (the 434 years), Gabriel says, "***And after*** *threescore and two weeks, shall Messiah be cut off, but not for himself..."* (emphasis added).

The words "*and after*" represent the *break* between weeks because Gabriel details what happens *after* the second set of weeks, but *before* the third and final week begins. In other words, Gabriel is saying that the first 7 weeks occur, immediately followed by the next 62 weeks, *and then* something happens. Note that it is not until verse 27, which states, *"And he shall confirm the covenant with many for one week..."* This reference to the "one week" that Wohlberg believes does *not* refer to the Tribulation actually *does* refer to the Tribulation.

Please understand that between the 69th week (7 weeks plus 62 weeks), there is an obvious *break* in the weeks. During this time:

- *Messiah will be cut off (killed)*
- *Destruction of the city and sanctuary (occurred in A.D. 70)*
- *Wars and rumors of wars until the end*

We know this represents a break because it is not until verse 27 that we read of a covenant that "he" enters into with "the many." Of course, theologians disagree over what the "he" and "the many" refer to, but it seems more in keeping with the rules of grammar to understand this particular "he" as referring back to first antecedent, which is "the prince to come." This prince to come is – *in my opinion* – the Antichrist. Wohlberg believes that all three instances of the use of the pronoun "he" in verse 27 refers back to the Messiah. However, since Gabriel referred to Messiah as just that – Messiah – and *never* with the use of a pronoun, it is doubtful that any of these uses of "he" refer to Messiah. Beyond this, Gabriel introduced a "prince to come" *after* referring to Messiah twice. It is most likely, then – if the rules of grammar mean anything – that the use of these pronouns refers to the prince to come, who is the Antichrist.

Wohlberg misapplies (in my opinion) the rules of grammar, stating that it is fine to say that all three instances of "he" in the later part of Daniel 9:24 – 27 refer to Messiah. In truth, by following the actual rules of grammar, we arrive at a different conclusion. Since the immediate "he" comes *after* Gabriel introduces "the prince who is to come," then it is much more reasonable to go back to the first antecedent, which is "the prince who is to come," not Messiah, the Prince.

If this is so, then it means that Antichrist enters into a covenant with "the many" for one week. This one week represents the final week of the 490 years (or 70 weeks), and is the last week, or final seven years. It is clear from the text that this covenant occurs at the very start of this last or 70th week. It is this covenant, then, which gives rise to the Tribulation.

Chapter 10

Oh, That Covenant...

Why is the covenant spoken of in Daniel 9:27 the *problem*? Why does *this* event bring about the Tribulation? Why, at this point, do PreTrib Rapturists and Dispensationalists believe that this event is *the* event that not only puts the Tribulation into gear, but also *invites* God to pour out His wrath onto Israel (essentially), as well as all unbelieving nations and people who have risen *against* Israel?

Bowing to Satan
By entering into a covenant with Antichrist, Israel has effectively *bowed* to Satan, something that Satan has wanted since before he fell

through pride. By signing on the dotted line with Antichrist, Israel has made the worst possible gaffe against God that could be done. They have *outwardly* begun to worship the devil, though they at this point are not aware of it.

In the Old Testament, there were many occasions where the Israelites abused God's good pleasure and forfeited fellowship with Him by bowing to *idols*. Most of us are likely very aware of the times in which Israel fell through idolatry, forsaking God.

In this particular case concerning the covenant signed with the Antichrist, Israel will in effect be signing a deal *directly* with Satan, since Paul tells us that this man of sin comes in *accord* with all the activity of Satan himself. This covenant, and Israel's agreement with it, will be the signatory event that causes God to pour out His wrath. Because of this, God's patience ends.

1. *He pours out His wrath onto Israel for their dereliction of responsibility as the nation He chose to be a light to the world.*
2. *He pours out His wrath on them because they have forsaken Him, their Creator and Protector, and*
3. *He pours out His wrath on them because they have entered into the worst possible form of idolatry imaginable; directly placing themselves under the power, promised provision and protection, and safety of Antichrist, instead of Jehovah God.*

This form of treason is reprehensible to God. It is bad enough to worship idols, but to deliberately *place trust* in Satan's man – effectively trusting in Satan himself – is to sin against God to the highest degree.

This action by "the many" in Israel leaves God no choice but to pour out His wrath on His disobedient and unrepentant *wife*. They are literally asking for it. In doing so, His wrath is also extended to those people and nations who have long set themselves against God's nation, *Israel*, and against God's chosen people, the *Israelites*. The plagues, the pestilences, the wars, the weather problems, the earthquakes, the strange signs in the skies – all of it – are God's wrath pouring out on this world.

God's Wrath is for *Unbelievers*
What the Antichrist does, chasing down and killing multitudes that will refuse to bow to him, is done *within* the will of God. He acts in accordance with God's will; however, he is acting based on his own *desires*. The entirety of the Tribulation is God's wrath. The Antichrist's actions toward those who either refuse to take the mark or who are believers are due solely to Antichrist's hatred of God's people. This "wrath" of the Antichrist, when poured out on *unbelievers,* is God's *wrath*. When poured out on *believers,* it is trials, persecutions, and tribulations, just as occurred through Nero and other potentates of long ago.

Gentiles routinely forget that had not Jesus been born into Israel (as a Jew), lived among that culture (as a Jew), learned the Scriptures (as a Jew), spoke, thought, and did all things *as a Jew*, even being rejected by His own people (as a Jew), there would be *no salvation* for Gentiles at all. It is because of Israel, because of the fact that Jesus came from Israel, and because of the fact that He – a full Jew by birth – could live among them, be counted among them, understand their culture and Scriptures, and ultimately be rejected and killed by them, that salvation is extended to *all* people and *all* nations.

Far from being angry with Jews or with Israel, we should praise God daily for them. At the same time, however, we must also be diligent in our witness *to them*, in order that the Lord of the Harvest might open their eyes to the truth that is only found in Him, so that many Jewish individuals *might* become Jewish *believers*. As Paul states in Romans, we owe a debt to the Jew. Without them there would be no salvation, because salvation (Jesus Christ) comes from the Jew. Do you see how this covenant with the Antichrist is such that it causes the final outpouring of God's wrath onto a wayward people and an unbelieving world?

Since the Church has already been purified (as Noah, Lot, Abraham and others were also purified because they believed God and it was counted to them as righteousness) through faith in God, the Church does *not* need to experience God's *wrath*. Many Posttribbers point to Noah, who was kept safe *within* God's wrath. No, Noah was kept safe completely *apart* from God's wrath. Neither Noah, nor any member of his family, or any animal on the Ark experienced any portion of God's wrath at any time, nor were they ever in danger of experiencing it.

Noah, Daniel, and the Boys
The Posttribber will say that this is their point: Noah was saved from the wrath of God by being kept safe *within* the Ark. Neither Noah and his family nor any of the animals were in *any* physical danger at *any* point during their time in the Ark. They were *completely safe* from all danger. In fact, one website states this without equivocation:

"Noah was not saved from the Flood, but through it.

Daniel was not saved from the lions' den, but through it.

Shadrach, Meshach, and Abed-Nego were not saved from the fiery furnace, but through it. In fact, Jesus went through it with them, and He will go through the great tribulation with us as well!

The children of Israel were not saved from Egypt before the plagues fell, but afterward. God demonstrated His love and power by preserving them in Egypt through the ten plagues. In the same way, the righteous will be in the world when the seven last plagues fall (Revelation 16), but God will preserve them."[11]

---

[11] http://www.bibleprophecytruth.com/topics/great-tribulation.aspx

The problems with the above statements are obvious to me. We will deal with Noah in detail shortly, but regarding Daniel, though he was thrown into the pit, he was not in any way harmed or attacked by any of the lions in the den with him. This is why Doug Batchelor (quoted above) makes the statement that these individuals were not saved *from* God's wrath, but *through it*. This seems to be splitting hairs. In none of the examples provided by Batchelor is *anyone* harmed in any way. Noah, Daniel, Shadrach, Meshach, Abednego, or any of the children of Israel were not harmed at all by any of the situations they found themselves in.

Because of this, folks like Batchelor (and Wohlberg as well, since they are both Seventh-day Adventists) and Posttribulationalists in general see them as being saved *through* the situation. However, if we consider the reality of the Tribulation, there is a guarantee that nearly *all* who enter it will die at some point during the time period. So what is Batchelor really meaning when he references Noah, Daniel, the three men in the fiery furnace or the children of Israel? Does he mean to say that as God saved these individuals, He will also save those who go through the Tribulation?

Batchelor comments on this by stating, *"Although God does not always provide an escape from tribulation, He does promise to give us the power and strength to get through it. 'I can do all things through Christ who strengthens me.' Philippians 4:13."*

Batchelor is Missing Some Important Points
Why, though, does Batchelor provide examples in which each case provides an *escape* from all potential physical harm? God did *much* more than merely save these individuals through the trials. He *completely protected* them from all of it. In fact, so free were they of any harm associated with these situations, that it was as if they were not even there at all. Granted, they did not necessarily know that this was God's plan (and in some cases, said as much). However, once

their trial began, it likely became immediately apparent that they were in no danger at all.

There is another point to be made here as well. Noah, Lot (not mentioned by Batchelor), and the children of Israel were deliberately *placed* in their respective situations by *God directly*.

- *God brought the Flood onto the earth in judgment (wrath).*
- *He destroyed Sodom and Gomorrah with fire and brimstone (wrath).*
- *The reason the children of Israel were not touched at all by anything that happened to Egypt was due to the fact that God sent those things on Egypt, not the children of Israel.*
- *All of the plagues (wrath) were conditioned upon the fact that Pharaoh stood against God in rebellion.*
- *The plagues were in no way intended for the Israelites at all. In essence, then, it was as if Israel was not even present during the plagues.*
- *If we consider Paul's words in Romans regarding these events, we read, "For the scripture saith unto Pharaoh, Even for this same purpose have I raised thee up, that I might shew my power in thee, and that my name might be declared throughout all the earth," (Romans 9:17, KJV).*

Read those words in Romans again, will you? God declares that *the* reason Pharaoh was raised up was that God was going to use him to show the power of His might and the glory of His Name throughout all the earth. This is *exactly* what God is going to do during the time of the Tribulation. He will display His *power* and His *might*, all for the *glory* of His Name. In fact, this is why there was the Flood, why He destroyed Sodom and Gomorrah, why He *allowed* Shadrach, Meshach, and Abednego to be thrown into the fire, why He allowed Daniel to be thrown into the lions' den, and why the Pharaoh reacted as he did. It was all for God's purposes. All for His glory. All for Him.

Saving Daniel, the three young men in the fire, Lot, Noah and the children of Israel was secondary. The first and foremost reason God saved them was so that He would receive the glory and honor that is due His Name.

The only plague in which the Israelites could have *possibly* been affected was during the Passover, and then only if they left their dwelling, either through unbelief or rebellion. They were warned beforehand that as long as they remained in their dwelling in which the doorposts and lintel were sprinkled with blood, the angel of death would pass over them.

That we take these examples and turn them around so that they appear to be done *for us* is ridiculous. The *only thing* that God promises to save me from is eternal destruction, because of the salvation that I have from Him. That is it. This is why there are Christians all over the world that have been and continue to be slaughtered one after the other. This world is governed by Satan, and God allows Him to do what He does in order that God will ultimately be glorified.

It appears to me that most, if not all, anti-PreTribbers simply fail to see the reason for any and all of the hardships that come to the Christian. They seem to think that the Tribulation period is simply "more of its kind."

What is THE Purpose for the Tribulation?
What they fail to see – in my opinion – is that the upcoming Tribulation has a special and unique purpose. It is the only Tribulation Jesus speaks of in which *the* final showdown between Satan and God takes place (and God will not even break into a proverbial sweat). It is the showdown of the century, and for that matter of all time. The Tribulation is *the* climax of everything God has stated, revealed, and worked toward from the beginning of our time. From Genesis 3, we read of the *eventual* battle between God and

Satan in which Satan is destroyed at the cross. The Tribulation is the time when God will begin carrying out that sentence.

This is what makes the upcoming Tribulation so incredibly unique and different from any *"tribulations, trials, persecutions, perils, or swords"* we might wind up experiencing in our short lives.

The normal, average life of each Christian is *not* this coming showdown. It is simply our Christian life, where Satan is allowed to create havoc in our lives *as God permits*. All of this is to His glory, though. Remember, *we* as human beings *invited* this havoc when we turned from God to ourselves as early as the Garden of Eden.

This planet is *fallen*. The animals are *fallen*. We remain *fallen*, but with a new nature within, a deposit from the Holy Spirit guaranteeing our eternal reward, and the guarantee of our physical death (unless Raptured first). This is true of authentic Christians.

As Christians, while we are here in this life there *will be* trials and tribulations that come our way. This is guaranteed by Christ and is the normal part of our existence, because we are *lights* shining out of the *darkness*. We are on the enemy's *home turf*. He is allowed *by God* to thwart, harass, hurt, and even kill us (solely at God's discretion), because this *is* Satan's territory and we are merely sojourning through it.

God could take each of His children home through an individual "rapture" when their time comes, instead of through death. Yet He has chosen not to do this, and it is strictly because of our fallen state that we physically die anyway. The fact that at some future point God may Rapture Christ's Church off this planet, as He "Raptured" a few of the Old Testament saints, is His business. Even *if* the PreTrib Rapture is guaranteed to occur, many of us alive today will not live to see it, being taken in physical death to our eternal home before that event occurs.

This is *not* at all the case for people *during* the Tribulation, who are under no such protection from God. Those opposed to the PreTrib Rapture need to consider two things, which I believe tend to negate the belief that Noah is actually a proof *for* their view of Posttribulationalism:

1. Because Noah was safely <u>inside</u> the Ark, there was absolutely no chance at all that **any** portion of God's wrath could ever touch him or the others within the Ark.
2. God's wrath resulted in the entire earth being completely enveloped in water, well above the highest mountain peak. This prevented God from keeping Noah and his family (or the animals) safe on <u>any portion</u> of the earth. There was no dry place left on the earth, since God was going to destroy every living thing on it with a global flood.

Considering these two points, then, understand that those who *become* Christians *during* the Tribulation will *always* be living with the possibility of experiencing *persecution* and even *death* because of their faith in Jesus. They will be alive during the unfortunate time when God has preordained that His final showdown with Satan (through the Antichrist) will occur.

Since it is God in Christ Jesus who directs the *start* of and the release of each trumpet, bowl, or seal, it is clearly signifying that these things are *from* God, therefore they represent *His* wrath poured out onto humanity.

First, for Noah, there was *no chance* that even a drop of water could touch him, unless he went *outside* the Ark of safety. Noah was completely safe *within* the Ark at all times. It wasn't that God merely saved Noah *through* anything. He completely *enveloped* Noah, placing Him inside a hermetically sealed Ark. Is that going to be the case for the Christians during the Tribulation? Hardly; and because of this, it is *impossible* to compare the two situations like that.

Eschatology Shouldn't Be a Fightin' Word!

As it was in the Days of Noah...

Noah, his family, and all animals were perfectly safe within the Ark <u>at all times</u>. There was never a chance of any portion of God's wrath touching them <u>at any time</u>. There is no such guarantee during the upcoming Tribulation for believers.

As Noah within the Ark literally <u>rose above the earth</u> during the global flood (God's wrath), the Church will rise above the earth in the Rapture, also avoiding all of God's wrath.

©2010 F. DERUVO

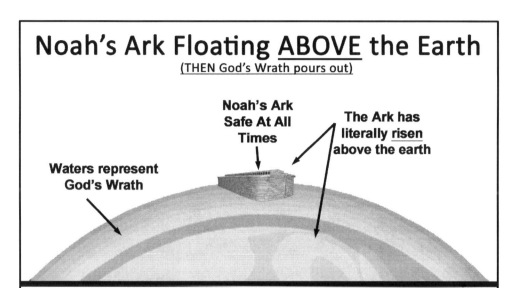

Secondly, if we understand that there was no place on God's earth where He could have placed Noah so that neither he nor his family would suffer any consequences from God's wrath pouring out, then we also need to understand that the *only* place God could have placed Noah was *on top of the water,* or literally <u>above</u> the earth. This kept Noah completely *out* of harm's way.

The Ark Rises Above the Earth
Being *above the earth* or *on top of* the water was the *only* place God had available to Him to be sure of Noah's safety. Yes, God *could* have taken Noah to heaven, along with his family and the animals, but why? What good would that have done? Had God done that, the results would have most likely been:

1. *Noah, his family and the animals would have had to <u>die</u>, since corruption cannot inherit incorruption*
2. *If Noah had died, he would not have been able to be placed back on earth in order to "be fruitful and replenish" it. Having died and gained an incorruptible body, Noah and his family would have lost the ability to reproduce.*

The *only* place that God could have put Noah was in a very large boat, which floated <u>over</u> the water, or literally <u>above the earth</u>. Once God's wrath was spent, the waters receded. Once they *completely* receded, Noah was able to leave the Ark, as did his family and the animals.

Once the Tribulation completes its run, so does God's *wrath*. His wrath ends when Jesus Christ returns, obliterates the Antichrist with the breath of His (Christ's) mouth, metes out His judgment, and begins His 1,000 year reign. We – His Bride – *return* with Him, to *reign* with Him.

Noah's Last Days
Ultimately, Noah lived his life *up to the flood* doing a number of things:

1. Building the Ark with his sons
2. Possibly preaching to, and warning people of the impending flood
3. Living each day as if it was his last day <u>outside</u> of the Ark
4. Doing all the normal things each of us does every day:
    a. Eating
    b. Sleeping
    c. Communicating
    d. Praying

In Genesis 6, we are officially introduced to Noah. God tells Noah He is not at all pleased with the way things were on the earth He created. He informs Noah about His solution to the problem.

"13 And God said unto Noah, The end of all flesh is come before me; for the earth is filled with violence through them; and, behold, I will destroy them with the earth.

14 Make thee an ark of gopher wood; rooms shalt thou make in the ark, and shalt pitch it within and without with pitch.

15 And this is the fashion which thou shalt make it of: The length of the ark shall be three hundred cubits, the breadth of it fifty cubits, and the height of it thirty cubits.

16 A window shalt thou make to the ark, and in a cubit shalt thou finish it above; and the door of the ark shalt thou set in the side thereof; with lower, second, and third stories shalt thou make it.

17 And, behold, I, even I, do bring a flood of waters upon the earth, to destroy all flesh, wherein is the breath of life, from under heaven; and every thing that is in the earth shall die.

18 But with thee will I establish my covenant; and thou shalt come into the ark, thou, and thy sons, and thy wife, and thy sons' wives with thee.

19 And of every living thing of all flesh, two of every sort shalt thou bring into the ark, to keep them alive with thee; they shall be male and female.

20 Of fowls after their kind, and of cattle after their kind, of every creeping thing of the earth after his kind, two of every sort shall come unto thee, to keep them alive.

21 And take thou unto thee of all food that is eaten, and thou shalt gather it to thee; and it shall be for food for thee, and for them.

22 Thus did Noah; according to all that God commanded him, so did he," (Genesis 6:13-22, KJV).

Why is God sharing any of this with Noah? If we refer back to verse 8 of this same chapter, we find these words: "*But Noah found grace in the eyes of the LORD.*" God saw Noah and He extended grace to him. Chuck Missler has pointed out in *Learn the Bible in 24 Hours* that it may well have had to do with the fact that his DNA had not been corrupted as the rest of humanity's had been. This had been accomplished through the intermingling of fallen angels with human women, forever changing the DNA that would be inherent within their offspring. Missler believes that Noah was somehow not affected by this, as none of his lineage had ever intermingled.

An Aside: Fallen Angels and Procreation
As a quick aside, some do not believe or accept the possibility that fallen angels (or any angels for that matter) could have found a way to cohabitate with human women. Maybe, but maybe not.

The real question is, what would Satan have gained by causing this to occur? The answer is simple. Had Satan successfully corrupted *all* human DNA, including Noah's, through his interbreeding program, how would a Messiah have been born? He also would have been equally *corrupted* due to the DNA that had been unalterably changed.

Noah's Timeline

God explains His plans to Noah. Tells him he has 120 years to build an Ark.

120 years later on an unknown day Noah enters the Ark. God seals it from the outside.

Seven days later God sends the deluge.

It rains 40 days/40 nights

God told Noah to prepare. He did, and he lived every day as his last knowing that God could call him into the Ark at any day or any hour. Once inside, God sealed him in, and all people and animals remained completely safe from any possible chance of experiencing any part of God's wrath.

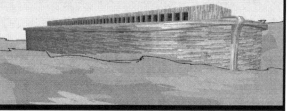

Sequence of Events for Noah

1. God tells Noah His plans
2. God will destroy all flesh
3. Noah is to build an Ark
4. Noah has 120 years to prepare
5. God CALLS Noah into the Ark
6. Exact time of God's CALLING was previously unknown to Noah
7. God seals the Ark from the outside
8. Everyone is completely safe within the Ark
9. The rains (God's WRATH) begin
10. The Ark rises ABOVE the earth
11. At no time are the occupants of the Ark in danger of God's wrath
12. At the end of God's wrath, Noah comes back to the earth

©2010 F. DERUVO

God tells Noah what He does not like where humanity is concerned, and what He is going to do about it. His plan includes Noah. Noah is told to build an Ark made of gopher wood. God gives Noah specific instructions regarding the height, depth, and length, and even to include a window, as well as a large door. God explains that there should be three levels to the ship, and it should be covered completely with pitch, making it fully sealed and waterproof. A global deluge was coming, and it would not be good to have the Ark take on water or sink.

Furthermore, God instructs Noah to bring in animals, and of course there would have been food for them as well as for himself and his family. In verse 22, we are told that Noah did *everything* God commanded.

From the time Noah was building the Ark until the time he was told by God to get into the Ark, a good deal of time passed. In fact, 120 years passed (cf. Genesis 6:3). Interestingly enough, even though Noah knew the length of time (120 years) before the end of the line for humanity would arrive, Noah did *not* know the actual *day* or *hour* when God would *call* him into the Ark.

As it happened, Noah was 600 years old when God said, "*Come thou and all thy house into the ark*," (Genesis 7:1b). God then announced that while Noah and the rest were in the Ark, after seven days God would open the heavens and pour water onto the earth for a period of 40 days and 40 nights. During the process, every living thing *outside* of the Ark would die, or in God's words, would be "destroyed." All within the Ark were completely safe and *never* in any danger of experiencing God's wrath – or any other peril, for that matter.

Once the flood was completely over and the waters had receded so that dry land was found, Noah, family and animals disembarked from the Ark. In essence, they *returned* to the earth after having been *removed* from it, just as the Rapture takes Christians off the earth and Christ returns *with* them at the end of the Tribulation.

Therefore, during the time leading up to the Global Flood, Noah continued to live with this coming devastation in mind. As he looked toward the future, this cataclysmic destruction was *always* before him. It was *because* of his awareness of the impending doom, along with the knowledge that he would escape from it, that *caused* him to live the way he lived. Chances are that he at least *tried* to warn others, preaching to them about the upcoming destruction.

In Spite of Knowing, Noah Did *Not* Grow Lazy
Because Noah knew the Flood was a foregone conclusion, he lived with this future truth, though he did not know the day or the hour he would be told to enter the Ark. The knowledge of this Flood provided him with the *impetus* to live accordingly. Far from sitting on his rear end doing nothing, Noah was *working*. He was involved in the work that the Lord had given him to do, which was primarily to build the Ark and gather supplies for it. That is hard work.

Imagine trying to build a ship roughly the size of the Queen Mary and you only have seven other men to help you. Though you have 120 years, it is *still* a great deal of work; but it needs to be done, and you do not balk at it. You do it. While you are doing that, you are cutting down trees, shaving off the bark, shaping the boards, and doing everything else that this huge project requires. The other normal things in life, like eating, sleeping and the rest are also still being done.

Had other human beings come up and wanted to know what was going on, you would tell them. Noah likely did this *if* people came up to him. But remember, if the entire human race had been corrupted because of the intermingling of fallen angels with human beings, chances are great that God wanted no other individuals saved. He simply wanted them destroyed. That would *not* stop Noah from telling them *what* he was doing, *why* he was doing it, and *when* this would all happen.

PreTrib Rapturists like me live with the Tribulation constantly before us. Even if it does not occur within our lifetimes, we know that the Tribulation *is* coming. We also believe that the PreTrib Rapture will occur *prior* to it – as it was in the days of *Noah*, and as it was in the days of *Lot*, so it is now. The Lord *warned*, He *took* His chosen completely *out of the way* so that they would not be harmed by His coming judgment, and *then* He proceeded to *release* His wrath onto the world. In essence,

1. *God warns*
2. *God removes*
3. *God pours out wrath*

The Formula Remains the Same
Whether it was the *Passover*, the *Flood*, or the destruction of *Sodom and Gomorrah*, the sequence is the *same*. As Christians, we are to be involved in God's work, and in this generation, His work involves the Great Commission. It involves telling people *what* Jesus Christ has done for them, and it involves explaining to them about salvation and that it is for all people; all people who *believe* on the Lord Jesus Christ will receive it.

This is what we are called to do. This is how we should live. The fact that there *is* a coming time of judgment simply makes it more *urgent*. If I am wrong about the timing of the Rapture, and it does not occur before the Tribulation, I will *not* lose my faith. I will not crumple to the ground, believing that God has "lied" to me. I have not yet lost my faith, in spite of the many difficult trials the Lord has seen fit to send my way. By His strength, I have gotten through each of them.

Instead, I will confess to Him that I was wrong. I will admonish myself and then I will get up *off* of my knees, grab my Bible and head out the door to do the same thing I do as a matter of course; share with people that God loves them and that His salvation is for all who believe. I will tell them that He came to die in order that they might have life, and if they will repent by changing their mind about who Jesus is, they are on their way to receiving His salvation.

While these events are supernatural, there is nothing *magical* about the Rapture or the Tribulation. I believe the Tribulation is a period of God's *final* wrath being poured out onto wayward *Israel* and all *unbelievers*. This final wrath takes place on this earth. He will do this to finally gain Israel's attention, chastising them for their centuries of disobedience. Beyond this, since God wants *no one* to perish, God will also work in the Tribulation, to allow His wrath to (hopefully) cause people to see their *need* for Him. Those who turn to Him will be saved. Those who do not will perish. Those who perish without Christ will ultimately be sent to the final wrath *off* the earth, which is never quenched.

The definitive reason for the Tribulation, I believe, is to show the universe for the last time that God is GOD, and there is none greater. While Satan has wanted God's throne for eons, God has been patient. During the Tribulation, God's patience will have ended. He will destroy Satan, his works, and, *unfortunately*, those who continue to worship him (Satan). The Tribulation is GOD's time! It is His preordained period of crushing the powers of darkness for the entire universe to witness. Those who errantly believe that only part of the Tribulation is God's wrath may very well be misunderstanding God's purpose for the Tribulation from the start.

What of <u>Believers</u> During the Tribulation?
Believers during the Tribulation will face situations that will try their faith, just as believers during the 20th century face these types of trials *daily* around the globe. Though they will grow through these experiences, none of these experiences will *perfect* them. In fact, Paul speaks of the truth that we are already perfect in Christ, already

complete and already seated with Him in the heavenly realm (cf. Ephesians 2). Only in death will they become perfected.

The Tribulation is unprecedented because of the *amount* and *tenaciousness* of God's wrath. Nothing that occurs during the Tribulation paints a pretty picture, with the exception of Christ's physical return to this earth.

As Jesus Himself said, this upcoming time of trouble is the worst this world will ever experience. Nothing like it has occurred before and nothing will occur after it. Noah lived each day leading up to entering the Ark as if it was his *last*. He knew it was simply a matter of time before God would call him to enter the Ark, along with his family and the animals. Far from making Noah spiritually immature or lazy, this knowledge created within him the *desire* to accomplish the tasks God had placed before him.

Noah *alone knew* that there was to be an upcoming time of judgment from which he would be saved. In light of this, how can some even possibly believe and claim that those of us who believe as Noah did will become *lazy, unspiritual, immature, carnally-minded* and all the other adjectives that are routinely tossed at PreTrib Rapturists?

The Bible provides at least *two* solid examples of how God revealed information about an upcoming time of judgment: Noah and Lot. In each case, but especially in the case of Noah, we see a man who knew of the Lord's upcoming judgment and *continued to work diligently* in the face of it. Christ deliberately used these examples in connection with the time surrounding His own Second Coming.

Lot – the (Righteous) Man!
Lot was a unique case altogether simply because it is clear from a human perspective that he was fairly *immature*. He had little to no control over his own family and it is doubtful that his relationship with God was anything much more than superficial. I cannot know

this for sure, but if we study his life and the *results* of it, it seems to tell us a good deal about the man.

The reality, though, is that Peter views Lot much differently (under the inspiration of the Holy Spirit) than we are tempted to see him. Lot was described as a righteous man! *"And delivered just Lot, vexed with the filthy conversation of the wicked: (For that righteous man dwelling among them, in seeing and hearing, vexed his righteous soul from day to day with their unlawful deeds;)"* (2 Peter 2:7-8, KJV).

Who would have thought? It is true. The one requirement of God – that we believe him – was obviously fulfilled by Lot, allowing God to credit Lot with righteousness.

By the time we get to Lot, prior to the destructive forces that God rains down on Sodom and Gomorrah, he is much older, probably a bit wiser, but it is clear that he has not had much of an impact on his family at all. During their escape, his wife turns to salt because she just *had* to look back at her home town. Lot's own daughters decided to get him drunk, and each took turns lying with him in order to become pregnant to continue the line. When we look at Lot it is not difficult to see someone who was not the most outwardly righteous person around, yet to God, Lot *was* righteous.

Lot did not receive much in the way of warning about this coming destruction on his city. The angels came, took the time to tell him about it, and then urged everyone to make haste, because they could not bring down destruction onto these two cities of the plain *until they got Lot out of harm's way*. It is that clear. God warned, He removed His righteous, *and then* He destroyed in His wrath.

Chapter 11
What is Spiritually Mature?

Obviously, the problem of people thinking that PreTrib Rapturists are *immature* is one that grates on those of us who *know* the struggles we go through, and how we work to submit ourselves to His will, just as anti-PreTribbers do. To date, I have never experienced a trial so bad that blood has been found to drip from my brow as if sweat. Then again, it is likely that you have not either. For that, we should both be grateful.

In fact, I have never experienced what Job from the Old Testament experienced either. While I *have* lost someone I love dearly (my sister), she was not taken in a tornado with the rest of my family.

The other things that Job experienced are not things that have visited me either. I have not experienced my teeth turning black and falling out. I have not developed sores and boils over my body which crushed me with extreme pain. I have not experienced my friends coming against me implying that I must have done something wrong to deserve this treatment. I have not had nights of insomnia, nor have I suffered from waking hallucinations. In short, I have not had Job's experience – and frankly, I do not want it. If the Lord sends those things to me, that's His business. For myself, I have checked my masochistic tendencies at the door.

Job's Experience
If, because of my lack of desire, you would accuse me of having an aversion to the type of suffering that Job experienced, then I would agree with you. Nevertheless, how does this make me any *less* spiritual? Do YOU have a *desire* to suffer for the Lord like that? Are you that much of a masochist? Do you feel that it is the best way possible to prove your love and dedication to Him? You might say, "*If the Lord wanted me to suffer like that, then I would.*" However, you did *not* answer the question. Do you WANT to suffer like that? I doubt it. If you do, then maybe something else is going on inside.

I'll be even more frank with you. I do *not* want to experience any pain when I die. I have an *aversion* to pain. I just don't like it one little bit. The reason I have an aversion to it is because I have experienced pain plenty of times. Each time, I am reminded *why* I do not enjoy it.

I am not one of these individuals who "gets off" on pain. I am not the stalwart soldier who trudges on in spite of his blisters, his thirst, his hunger and his fatigue. Does this make me *less* spiritual than you?

Rate Yourself
Conversely, let me ask something of all of you folks who believe that PreTrib Rapturists have an absolute *aversion* to suffering "for the

Lord." Here is the question: if you look back over all the painful experiences of your life, how would you rate your ability to muscle through them? *Good, bad, or ugly?*

People who speak of the PreTrib Rapturist having this supposed aversion to suffering through the Tribulation sound a bit judgmental to me. They obviously assume that I am not acquainted with *pain*, with *persecution*, or with *suffering*. How *dare* anyone say that of another Christian! This is what they said of Paul, who took the time to *list* the numerous things that he did suffer for the Lord. The fact that he felt he had to share it (as if bragging), caused him to say *"I must be out of my mind talking like this!"* (cf. 2 Corinthians 11)

I could list many times in my life when I experienced real persecutions or the pain of losing a loved one. I could discuss the times I have felt completely abandoned *by everyone,* yet forced myself to believe that God had *not* abandoned me. I could take the time to list the travails, the heartache and the terrible times (from an outward perspective) that have visited me in my lifetime. I could also point to those same times as opportunities for *growth,* because that is what they *produced*. I could also point to the Lord's *faithfulness* in each of these situations, in spite of how I was tempted to view each of them.

In short, my life – *like yours* – has been filled with trials, tribulations, and persecutions. There have also been numerous times of chastisement and, believe it or not, I look back even on *those* times fondly because it proves how much God loves me (cf. Hebrews 12:6).

God loves *me*. He absolutely, unfailingly loves *me*, in spite of how often I fail *Him*. He loves me and already sees me as *completed*, *perfected* in Him, though my living experience is often *far* from that. God loves *me* and He loves you the *exact* same way.

A Big Faux Pas
Just recently, I recall a time when I had done something that was

sinful. God took the time to chastise me for it. Do you know what it felt like? It felt like I had made God cry. It felt like I had *grieved* the Holy Spirit. I felt terrible. I felt as if I would do anything I could do to make it right. One thing I noticed was that through this situation, I did not once feel *guilty*. I felt sad, terribly, terribly sad, and filled with sorrow and remorse. I quickly confessed to Him, telling Him over and over how sorry I was. I simply remember saying, *"Lord God, I am so sorry. I am so sorry that I did this. I am so sorry that I caused you hurt. I am so sorry. Please God, help me to correct this situation so that you might be glorified because of it. Please, my Father and my God, help me to do what was right."*

The situation was *financial* and as the head of the home, I had made a very stupid, stupid (did I say *stupid*?) decision that created a major problem and financial hardship for us. When I realized it, I realized that I had run ahead of God. I was astounded to see that in my own pigheadedness, I had failed to turn to Him in prayer and *wait for direction*. I resolved to do it my way and *did*, reaping the consequences of my stupidity and unfaithfulness. I was completely remorseful and God knew it. My confession to Him was real. My thankfulness for His forgiveness was genuine, and because of it He created within me much more humility, and He developed more of Christ's character within me. That may sound like bragging, but believe me, it's not. I did *not* say that I became *completely humble* or that *Christ's character was perfectly created within me because of it*. I said His chastisement caused *growth*.

All the people who constantly and consistently believe that because of my belief in the PreTrib Rapture I am one who has an aversion to suffering are really doing nothing more than allowing their own *pride* to well up within them and speak for them. They are saying that *they* would not shrink from suffering. *They* would give their *all* for the Lord, not shy away like the "phony" PreTrib Rapturist. Well, my friend and brother/sister, it would be well for you to stop and recognize pride growing within you *before* the Lord has to bring it to your attention. If He brings it to your attention, you and I both know that it will not necessarily be a pleasant situation at all.

If we doubt this, all we need do is go to 2 Samuel 12 to see how, since David was so unable to see his own sin, God had to send Nathan to open David's eyes. The consequences remain, in spite of the fact that David repented, confessed, and received God's forgiveness.

We *all* need to be in constant humility before the Lord, or He will take us to task for it.

Chapter 12

What is an Authentic Christian?

Aside from the fact that it takes authentic salvation to actually *be* a Christian, beyond that what does it mean to be a Christian where the rubber meets the road? In other words, as I go through each day, how do I *live* each of those 24 hours? How do I deal with the situations that occur in my life *daily* that are not altogether *pleasant*?

At the risk of being ridiculed by those who, after reading this far in this book, are still unconvinced of my integrity, I will share what I *do* and how I endeavor to *apply* God's truth to all situations. Please understand that like you, I do none of this perfectly.

Being Thankful for *Everything* (and He Means *Everything*)
We are told that we should give thanks to God for *everything*, because this is *His* will concerning us, correct (cf. 1 Thessalonians 5:18)? If so, then we must take this admonition *seriously*. If we take the time to give thanks for each situation that comes our way, then what are we really doing?

If we are authentically *praising* God for *everything*, then we *are* unequivocally *submitting* to Him. If we are *submitting* to Him, then we are *yearning* for and *expecting* spiritual growth to occur, regardless of the cost.

It is *impossible* to authentically submit to Him *without* growing from that submission. I have found that for me, the best, and at times the most *efficient* way, to submit to Him is by immediately entering into an attitude of praise to Him for the *situation*, whatever it may be. It is in praising Him that I believe we are made to *immediately* come to grips with *His* will, *bypassing* ours.

Often, when difficult situations come to us, our first impulse is to run from them. We *all* do that. We want to *push* them away because it does not feel good. The worse the situation, the worse we feel about it and the less we *want* that situation around.

Of course, God may have other ideas entirely. Remember, once we *received* salvation we entered into a process Paul refers to as sanctification (Romans 6ff). This process lasts the *remainder* of our time on earth. It is the process of perfecting us, but we will *never* become perfected in this life. It is only when we stand before Him in glory that we will finally come into the perfection that He has set aside for us.

The process of sanctification is one in which we are constantly being tested under various trials of our faith. These trials are meant to create a spiritual maturity within us as we learn to receive what God sends us. The best way to receive whatever God sends our way is to do it with *praise* and *thanksgiving,* in spite of how we feel about the situation. Even if we begin to praise Him, even though we do not *feel* like it, He will soon take that sacrificial offer and praise and allow us to overcome the feelings of despair *within* that situation.

This is the surest way to inform our "old man," or flesh, that we are serious about praising God in all things and submitting our will to His. I'm not trying to put this forth as a formula. I'm simply saying that as difficult as it is, we should immediately begin to praise God for all situations that occur in our life, because this is the best way to acknowledge that we believe God has every aspect of our life in His *care.* If we "kick against the goads," so to speak, we will be acting difficult, immature, and will likely do more damage to others and ourselves in the process. God will have to continue to send situations like that in order to help us grow past it. If we adopt an attitude of praise right from the start, then it is actually easier to *give up our own desires* in exchange for *His, due to our willingness to* praise Him.

Paul and Barnabas

There are many wonderful examples of this in Scripture, but let me just highlight one of them. In the book of Acts, Paul and Barnabas were thrown in prison because Paul had exorcised a girl whose owner received a good deal of money from her "talent." She was possessed, but obviously the man who owned her did not care about that. He only cared that he had lost his source of *income.* The owner of the slave girl brought charges against both Paul and Barnabas and they were unmercifully thrown into prison.

Now what is interesting here is that neither Paul nor Barnabas hung their heads in despair. They did not go, *"oh, woe is me!"* They did not ask in an accusatory fashion, *"Where are you, God?!"* What they *did* was to immediately enter into prayer *and sing praises to God* (cf. Acts 16:25). What was the result? Well, in *their* case, an earthquake occurred, breaking open the jail cell doors and breaking their chains from the wall. Did they sing praises to God in hopes of Him breaking them out of prison? I don't think so at all. I think they sang praises to God because they firmly believed that what had happened to them was *His* will for them. They were not sure of the outcome, but they *were* sure that whatever happened did so because it was the Lord's will for them.

I'm sure they did not sit there with their feet in the stocks, chained to the wall, thinking, "*Hey, let's start praising the Lord and* **maybe** *an earthquake or something will happen and break us free from these stocks and this prison!*" I firmly believe that they wanted to praise God anyway *because* of the fact that His will had *happened to them already*. They were sure of it, and on that basis alone He was worthy to be praised.

Nevertheless, what was the *larger* outcome of their praising God? Yes, an earthquake occurred, and with it, their feet were free of the stocks, their arms were no longer chained to the walls and the jail cell doors opened. At that point, the jailer came running in, and seeing what had happened, with all the prisoners accounted for, asked a simple question. "*Sirs, what must I do to be saved?*" (Acts 16:30b) It would appear that God's plan included *salvation* for this jailer. Do you think either Paul or Barnabas knew that ahead of time? Nope.

Let's look at the events as they occurred in Acts 16. Paul and Barnabas went to the city of Thyatira to preach the Gospel. Once there, that is exactly what they did. As they preached the Gospel, a servant girl, possessed of a demon, heard what Paul and Barnabas preached and started to *agree* with them.

Obviously, demons know truth when they hear it. However, the demon within the girl began to act as a herald or announcer for them. It started to turn into a sideshow with the servant girl as a sideshow barker.

Beyond this, even though the demon was *telling* the truth, the last thing Paul wanted was a demon "on their side." Paul wanted the powers of darkness to have nothing to do with the Lord's work of evangelization in Thyatira, or anywhere else! The Spirit led him to do something about it, so he *did*.

Is Casting Out the Same as Stealing?
When Paul cast out the demon, it took away the source of income for the owner. The owner wanted some type of recompense, but since Paul and Barnabas had nothing, he had them put into debtor's prison. Let the authorities deal with them and at least remove their freedom. While there, Paul and Barnabas prayed and sang praises to God. The result was a jailer who became a new creation in Christ!

Therefore, it would appear that the demon was placed *inside* that girl, and that girl was placed right *behind* Paul and Barnabas, so that Paul would *call* the demon out of her. This set a chain reaction into place that ultimately *brought* one soul (and his entire family) into the kingdom of God! Who knows how many others believed after that because of the jailer's salvation?

Now, had Paul and Barnabas started complaining instead of singing, or had they gotten angry at the situation and kept asking, "*Why, God?*" then chances are very good that things would have been different. I do not believe for a moment that the jailer would *not* have ultimately been saved. He was saved because he was chosen to be saved from eternity past. Had Paul and Barnabas *not* done what they *should* have done, the Jailer would have eventually *been* saved somehow, some way.

The good news is that the Jailer *was* saved, and the events that immediately led up to it occurred because of *how* Paul and Barnabas reacted to *their* situation. They had no foreknowledge that God was planning to use their imprisonment to bring the jailer to salvation. They had no clue at all. That did not matter. What Paul and

Barnabas were looking at was the fact that they *believed* they were in prison *because* it was God's will, and that was that. Because it was God's will, they were going to praise Him for it.

I have gone through many trials and trying times in my life. I am almost 53 years of age, and within the past decade especially, my body has begun the process of wearing out. I have had surgery on my shoulder, and I have suffered (and continue to suffer from) a skin disorder that is incurable. Currently, it is in remission, and though it is not a cancer of any type and cannot kill me, it is uncomfortable to say the least when it flares up.

Beyond this, my doctor has told me that I now need foot surgery because I have developed a bone spur on my heel. It is painful and I limp a good deal until my ligaments get warmed up.

Moreover, I have experienced the normal amount of family difficulties with my parents (my father is deceased), which has really affected me emotionally over the years. The Lord has been so kind in healing a great deal, though. I lost my one and only sibling to two really strange diseases that I had never heard of before, and it was extremely sudden. Though she is with the Lord, I miss her.

I have also had my share of spiritual troubles; some caused by myself, but others that simply came to me under the Lord's direction. At least a few of these situations seemed unbearable at the time. God brought me through each one, and I like to think that I am wiser, stronger spiritually, and more spiritually mature because of them.

I won't bore you with any more details or instances. Suffice it to say that like you, I have definitely had my share of Christian growing pains, and through all of them I *know* that God has been at work. He has been perfecting me, recreating Christ's character within me and helping me deny myself in order that I might embrace more of Him. I also know that when I have taken the time to praise Him for everything (and I mean everything), I am able to embrace that situation much more quickly than through any other means.

I believe that as I continue to live the rest of my life one day at a time, I will do so with my eyes on the prize of receiving the Crown of Life. I firmly believe that the Tribulation is not that far down the road ahead of me. Prior to that, I believe Christ *will* call His Bride home in the Rapture. I may, however, *not* live to see it. He may already have the remainder of my physical days on this earth ending sometime *before* the Rapture happens.

It absolutely does *not* matter. What matters is that I live *for* Him, by giving *up* myself. Every time I praise Him, I die more and more to my selfish desires and I embrace more and more of His will. Whether I live another day, a year, five years or longer, and whether I am alive when the Rapture happens or not, the plain truth of the matter is that no authentic Christian can say that he or she loves God if they are not *serving* Him daily. No authentic Christian can be serving Him if he or she is not *dying* to self and embracing His will for their lives.

This is what we are *called* to do. This is how we are called to *live*. We become His servants because He bought us with the preciousness of His perfect, innocent blood, shed for us. If we truly love Him, we will yearn to become *indentured* servants to His purposes and His will. We will do this in order that He will be glorified in all things. There is no other way to do it, as far as I know. Whether I live or die, I want to say with Paul that I do all *for* Christ.

Death or Rapture
The PreTrib Rapture is ultimately *nothing*, really, in and of itself (and neither is any other Rapture supposition). It is a *vehicle*, which takes us from this life to His presence in the twinkling of an eye *without* experiencing death. Death also removes us from this life to His presence in the twinkling of an eye, though unfortunately there is often *pain* associated with it, unlike the Rapture.

In the end, though, it does *not* matter to me whether I *die* or I am *raptured* into His presence. If the Rapture is a figment of my imagination, then it is a figment of my imagination. What that means is that *if* I am alive when the Tribulation starts, I will go through at least *part* of the Tribulation before my life is taken from me. At some point I may very well be asked to recant my faith, if I have not already been taken by some pestilence, famine, or war. In Him, I will remain stalwart.

Living with Christ – the Ultimate Goal for the Christian
I believe that, though the times of the coming Tribulation will be horrific in scale, as Jesus stated in the Olivet Discourse, if I am alive to that point, then God *will* preserve me through it, <u>*spiritually*</u>. I have no doubt of that, and though I may lose my life in the process, who cares? I will simply be ushered into His presence. What could possibly be *better* than that? How could I *possibly* view that as a *problem*? Not only is it *not* a problem, but it is truly what I live for – to *see* Him, to be *like* Him, to *worship* Him in absolute spirit and truth, all <u>*in person*</u>. Who really cares *how* I get to heaven, or how I am brought into His presence? The fact that I will be brought into His presence at all is enough for me.

May he be pleased with this book and be *glorified* because of it. May authentic Christians learn to stop bickering over incidentals that really amount to nothing. May we concentrate on bringing Him glory in everything we *do*, everything we *say*, and everything we *think*. May God be praised in all things and above all things.

> *"Blessed is the man that walketh not in the counsel of the ungodly, nor standeth in the way of sinners, nor sitteth in the seat of the scornful. But his delight is in the law of the LORD; and in his law doth he meditate day and night. And he shall be like a tree planted by the rivers of water, that bringeth forth his fruit in his season; his leaf also shall not wither; and whatsoever he doeth shall prosper,"* (Psalms 1:1-3, KJV)

Chapter 13
One Final Thought...

Most of us have seen the illustration above left, since it has been around for decades. What do *you* see when you look at it? How about the one on the right?

In the one on the left, depending on how you view it, either you will see a young woman facing away from the viewer or you will see an old woman's profile. Let's say that you see the young woman, but your friend only sees the old woman. You both insist that only *what you see* is correct. You might even make a statement like, *"Look, the only thing that is in that illustration is the (young/old) woman, period! What you are seeing is simply not there."*

For the one on the right, do you see a saxophone player or the front of a woman's face? You *may* get to a point where you will see *both* things in both illustrations.

We need to approach God and His Word with absolute humility, knowing that what is most important is *His* meaning, *not* ours. To make declarative statements when there is theological wiggle room is to dismiss conversation and judge others. We can afford to do neither. ■

BOOKS:

- The Anti-Supernatural Bias of "Ex-Christians," by Fred DeRuvo
- The Basis of the Premillennial Faith, by Charles C. Ryrie
- Biblical Hermeneutics, by Milton S. Terry
- The Christian and Social Responsibility, by Charles C. Ryrie
- The Church in Prophecy, by John F. Walvoord
- Dictionary of Premillennial Theology, Mal Couch, Editor
- Dispensationalism Tomorrow & Beyond, by Christopher Cone, Editor
- Exploring the Future, by John Phillips
- Footsteps of the Messiah, by Arnold G. Fruchtenbaum
- Future Israel (Why Christian Anti-Judaism Must Be Challenged), by E. Ray Clendenen, Ed.
- Interpreting the Bible, by A. Berkeley Mickelsen
- Interpreting the Bible (is not as confusing as it seems), Fred DeRuvo
- Israelology, by Arnold G. Fruchtenbaum
- The Moody Handbook of Theology, by Paul Enns
- The Mountains of Israel, by Norma Archbold
- The Pre-Wrath Rapture Answered, by Lee W. Brainard
- Prolegomena, by Christopher Cone
- The Promises of God, a Bible Survey, by Christopher Cone
- Some Posttribulationists Say the Darndest Things, by Fred DeRuvo
- There Really Is a Difference! by Renald Showers
- Things to Come, by J. Dwight Pentecost
- The Truth War, by John MacArthur
- What on Earth is God Doing? By Renald Showers

Resources for Your Library (cont'd)

INTERNET:

- Anti-Preterist Blog — antipreterist.wordpress.com
- Ariel Ministries — www.ariel.org
- Berean Watchmen — www.bereanwatchmen.com
- Foothill Bible Church — www.foothill-bible.org
- Friends of Israel — www.foi.org
- Grace to You — www.gty.org
- Prophezine — www.prophezine.com
- Prophecy in the News — www.prophecyinthenews.com
- Study-Grow-Know — www.studygrowknow.com
- Study-Grow-Know Blog — www.modres.wordpress.com
- Tyndale Theological Seminary — www.tyndale.edu

Find more of Fred DeRuvo's books at the following places:

- Prophecy in the News — www.prophecyinthenews.com
- Study-Grow-Know — www.studygrowknow.com
- Amazon — www.amazon.com
- CreateSpace — www.createspace.com

Listen to *Study-Grow-Know* on the following stations:

Dr. Fred DeRuvo is heard weekly, every Saturday morning at Noon on **AM 950 KAHI**. Those who are out of the broadcast area have the option of going to **www.kahi.com** and hearing the show live at Noon, or any time from the Audio On-Demand section of their Web site!

Head on over to **live365.com** and search for "study grow know" to hear Dr. DeRuvo there as well.

Study-Grow-Know is a program that highlights religion, society, and politics in these End Times. Each broadcast tackles a specific subject that is important to those interested in knowing more about how the events of our world may be fulfilling Bible prophecy. Dr. DeRuvo avoids the sensationalism that many prophecy teachers fall into, presenting facts and Scripture.

Eschatology Shouldn't Be a Fightin' Word!

The following books from Dr. DeRuvo are in-progress and starting with *End of the Ages* (commentary on Revelation), should be available soon. For the latest information, stay tuned to **www.studygrowknow.com** for all the updates.

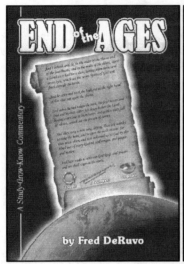  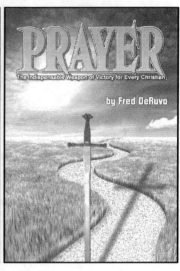

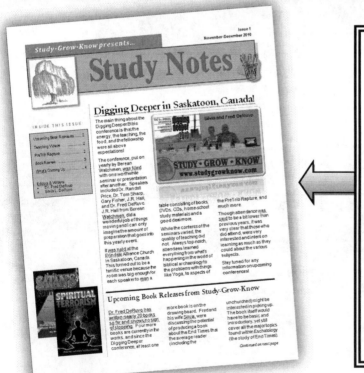

Sign up to receive our e-news, published six times per year. There is no cost involved as the 4 – 8 page newsletter is sent via e-mail. Just send us your e-mail address with a request to receive Study Notes!

Made in the USA
Charleston, SC
20 March 2012